Against War and In Praise of Folly
By Desiderius Erasmus
Edited by Anthony Uyl

Woodstock, Ontario, 2017

Against War and In Praise of Folly

Against War and In Praise of Folly
By Desiderius Erasmus
Edited by Anthony Uyl

Copyrights: Against War 1907, In Praise of Folly 1688

The text of "Against War" and the text of "In Praise of Folly" are all in the Public Domain. The layout is not in the Public Domain and is Copyright 2017© Devoted Publishing a division of 2165467 Ontario Inc.

Let us hear your stories and thoughts!

Contact us at: devotedpub@hotmail.com
Visit us on Facebook: @DevotedPublishing
Visit our website: www.devotedpublishing.com

Published in Woodstock, Ontario, Canada 2017.

For bulk and educational rates, contact at the email address above!

ISBN: 978-1-988297-87-3

Table of Contents

Against War 4
   INTRODUCTION 5
   DULCE BELLUM INEXPERTIS 11
In Praise of Folly 26
   Erasmus of Rotterdam to his friend 27
   THE PRAISE OF FOLLY 29

Against War

By Desiderius Erasmus
With an Introduction by J·W· MacKail

Originally Published by:
The Merrymount Press Boston, MDCCCCVII; Copyright, 1907, by D. B. Updike

Desiderius Erasmus

INTRODUCTION

The Treatise on War, of which the earliest English translation is here reprinted, was among the most famous writings of the most illustrious writer of his age. Few people now read Erasmus; he has become for the world in general a somewhat vague name. Only by some effort of the historical imagination is it possible for those who are not professed scholars and students to realize the enormous force which he was at a critical period in the history of civilization. The free institutions and the material progress of the modern world have alike their roots in humanism. Humanism as a movement of the human mind culminated in the age, and even in a sense in the person, of Erasmus. Its brilliant flower was of an earlier period; its fruits developed and matured later; but it was in his time, and in him, that the fruit set! The earlier sixteenth century is not so romantic as its predecessors, nor so rich in solid achievement as others that have followed it. As in some orchard when spring is over, the blossom lies withered on the grass, and the fruit has long to wait before it can ripen on the boughs. Yet here, in the dull, hot midsummer days, is the central and critical period of the year's growth.

The life of Erasmus is accessible in many popular forms as well as in more learned and formal works. To recapitulate it here would fall beyond the scope of a preface. But in order to appreciate this treatise fully it is necessary to realize the time and circumstances in which it appeared, and to recall some of the main features of its author's life and work up to the date of its composition.

That date can be fixed with certainty, from a combination of external and internal evidence, between the years 1513 and 1515; in all probability it was the winter of 1514-15. It was printed in the latter year, in the "editio princeps" of the enlarged and rewritten Adagia then issued from Froben's great printing-works at Basel. The stormy decennate of Pope Julius II had ended in February, 1513. To his successor, Giovanni de' Medici, who succeeded to the papal throne under the name of Leo X, the treatise is particularly addressed. The years which ensued were a time singularly momentous in the history of religion, of letters, and of the whole life of the civilized world. The eulogy of Leo with which Erasmus ends indicates the hopes then entertained of a new Augustan age of peace and reconciliation. The Reformation was still capable of being regarded as an internal and constructive force, within the framework of the society built up by the Middle Ages. The final divorce between humanism and the Church had not yet been made. The long and disastrous epoch of the wars of religion was still only a dark cloud on the horizon. The Renaissance was really dead, but few yet realized the fact. The new head of the Church was a lover of peace, a friend of scholars, a munificent patron of the arts. This treatise shows that Erasmus, to a certain extent, shared or strove to share in an illusion widely spread among the educated classes of Europe. With a far keener instinct for that which the souls of men required, an Augustinian monk from Wittenberg, who had visited Rome two years earlier, had turned away from the temple where a corpse lay swathed in gold and half hid in the steam of incense. With a far keener insight into the real state of things, Machiavelli was, at just this time, composing The Prince.

In one form or another, the subject of his impassioned pleading for peace among beings human, civilized, and Christian, had been long in Erasmus's mind. In his most celebrated single work, the Praise of Folly, he had bitterly attacked the attitude towards war habitual, and evilly consecrated by usage, among kings and popes. The same argument had formed the substance of a document addressed by him, under the title of Anti-Polemus, to Pope Julius in 1507. Much of the substance, much even of the phraseology of that earlier work is doubtless repeated here. Beyond the specific reference to Pope Leo, the other notes of time in the treatise now before us are few and faint. Allusions to Louis XII of France (1498-1515), to Ferdinand the Catholic (1479-1516), to Philip, king of Aragon (1504-1516), and Sigismund, king of Poland (1506-1548), are all consistent with the composition of the treatise some years earlier. At the end of it he promises to treat of the matter more largely when he publishes the Anti-Polemus. But this intention was never carried into effect. Perhaps Erasmus had become convinced of its futility; for the events of the years which followed soon showed that the new Augustan age was but a false dawn over which night settled more stormily and profoundly than before.

For ten or a dozen years Erasmus had stood at the head of European scholarship. His name was as famous in France and England as in the Low Countries and Germany. The age was indeed one of those in which the much-abused term of the republic of letters had a real and vital meaning. The nationalities of modern Europe had already formed themselves; the notion of the Empire had become obsolete, and if the imperial title was still coveted by princes, it was under no illusion as to the amount of effective supremacy which it carried with it, or as to any life yet remaining in the mediaeval doctrine of the unity of Christendom whether as a church or as a state. The discovery of the new world near the end of the previous century precipitated a revolution in European politics towards which events had long been moving, and finally broke up the political framework of the Middle Ages. But the other great event of the same period, the invention and diffusion of the art of printing, had created a new European commonwealth of the mind. The history of the century which followed it is a history in which the landmarks are found less in battles and treaties than in books.

The earlier life of the man who occupies the central place in the literary and spiritual movement of his time in no important way differs from the youth of many contemporary scholars and writers. Even the illegitimacy of his birth was an accident shared with so many others that it does not mark him out in any way from his fellows. His early education at Utrecht, at Deventer, at Herzogenbosch; his enforced and unhappy novitiate in a house of Augustinian canons near Gouda; his secretaryship to the bishop of Cambray, the grudging patron who allowed rather than assisted him to complete his training at the University of Paris--all this was at the time mere matter of common form. It is with his arrival in England in 1497, at the age of thirty-one, that his effective life really begins.

For the next twenty years that life was one of restless movement and incessant production. In England, France, the Low Countries, on the upper Rhine, and in Italy, he flitted about gathering up the whole intellectual movement of the age, and pouring forth the results in that admirable Latin which was not only the common language of scholars in every country, but the single language in which he himself thought instinctively and wrote freely. Between the Adagia of 1500 and the Colloquia of 1516 comes a mass of writings equivalent to the total product of many fertile and industrious pens. He worked in the cause of humanism with a sacred fury, striving with all his might to connect it with all that was living in the old and all that was developing in the newer world. In his travels no less than in his studies the aspect of war must have perpetually met him as at once the cause and the effect of barbarism; it was the symbol of everything to which humanism in its broader as well as in its narrower aspect was utterly opposed and repugnant. He was a student at Paris in the ominous year of the first French invasion of Italy, in which the death of Pico della Mirandola and Politian came like a symbol of the death of the Italian Renaissance itself. Charles VIII, as has often been said, brought back the Renaissance to France from that expedition; but he brought her back a captive chained to the wheels of his cannon. The epoch of the Italian wars began. A little later (1500) Sandro Botticelli painted that amazing Nativity which is one of the chief treasures of the London National Gallery. Over it in mystical Greek may still be read the painter's own words: "This picture was painted by me Alexander amid the confusions of Italy at the time prophesied in the Second Woe of the Apocalypse, when Satan shall be loosed upon the earth." In November, 1506, Erasmus was at Bologna, and saw the triumphal entry of Pope Julius into the city at the head of a great mercenary army. Two years later the league of Cambray, a combination of folly, treachery and shame which filled even hardened politicians with horror, plunged half Europe into a war in which no one was a gainer and which finally ruined Italy: "bellum quo nullum," says the historian, "vel atrocius vel diuturnius in Italia post exactos Gothos majores nostri meminerunt." In England Erasmus found, on his first visit, a country exhausted by the long and desperate struggle of the Wars of the Roses, out of which she had emerged with half her ruling class killed in battle or on the scaffold, and the whole fabric of society to reconstruct. The Empire was in a state of confusion and turmoil no less deplorable and much more extensive. The Diet of 1495 had indeed, by an expiring effort towards the suppression of absolute anarchy, decreed the abolition of private war. But in a society where every owner of a castle, every lord of a few square miles of territory, could conduct public war on his own account, the prohibition was of little more than formal value. Humanism had been introduced by the end of the fifteenth century in some of the German universities, but too late to have much effect on the rising fury of religious controversy. The very year in which this treatise against war was published gave to the world another work of even wider circulation and more profound consequences. The famous Epistolae Obscurorum Virorum, first published in 1515, and circulated rapidly among all the educated readers of Europe, made an open breach between the humanists and the Church. That breach was never closed; nor on the other hand could the efforts of well-intentioned reformers like Melancthon bring humanism into any organic relation with the reformed movement. When mutual exhaustion concluded the European struggle, civilization had to start afresh; it took a century more to recover the lost ground. The very idea of humanism had long before then disappeared.

War, pestilence, the theologians: these were the three great enemies with which Erasmus says he had throughout life to contend. It was during the years he spent in England that he was perhaps least harassed by them. His three periods of residence there--a fourth, in 1517, appears to have been of short duration and not marked by any very notable incident--were of the utmost importance in his life. During the first, in his residence between the years 1497 and 1499 at London and Oxford, the English Renaissance, if the name be fully applicable to so partial and inconclusive a movement, was in the promise and ardour of its brief spring. It was then that Erasmus made the acquaintance of those great Englishmen whose names cannot be mentioned with too much reverence: Colet, Grocyn, Latimer, Linacre. These men were the makers of modern England to a degree hardly realized. They carried the future in their hands. Peace had descended upon a weary country; and the younger generation was full of new hopes. The Enchiridion Militis Christiani, written soon after Erasmus returned to France, breathes the spirit of one who had not lost hope in the reconciliation of the Church and the world, of the old and new. When Erasmus made his second visit to England, in 1506, that fair promise had grown and spread. Colet had become dean of Saint Paul's; and through him, as it would appear, Erasmus now made the acquaintance of another great man with whom he soon formed as close an intimacy, Thomas More.

His Italian journey followed: he was in Italy nearly three years, at Turin, Bologna, Venice, Padua, Siena, Rome. It was in the first of these years that Albert Dürer was also in Italy, where he met Bellini and was recognized by the Italian masters as the head of a new transalpine art in no way inferior to their own. The year after Erasmus left Italy, Botticelli, the last survivor of the ancient world, died at Florence.

Meanwhile, Henry VIII, a prince, young, handsome, generous, pious, had succeeded to the throne of England. A golden age was thought to have dawned. Lord Mountjoy, who had been the pupil of Erasmus at Paris, and with whom he had first come to England, lost no time in urging Henry to send for the most brilliant and famous of European scholars, and attach him to his court. The king, who had already met and admired him, needed no pressing. In the letter which Henry himself wrote to Erasmus entreating him to take up his residence in England, the language employed was that of sincere admiration; nor was there any conscious insincerity in the main motive which he urged. "It is my earnest wish," wrote the king, "to restore Christ's religion to its primitive purity." The history of the English Reformation supplies a strange commentary on these words.

But the first few years of the new reign (1509-1513), which coincide with the third and longest sojourn of Erasmus in England, were a time in which high hopes might not seem unreasonable. While Italy was ravaged by war and the rest of Europe was in uneasy ferment, England remained peaceful and prosperous. The lust of the eyes and the pride of life were indeed the motive forces of the court; but alongside of these was a real desire for reform, and a real if very imperfect attempt to cultivate the nobler arts of peace, to establish learning, and to purify religion. Colet's great foundation of Saint Paul's School in 1510 is one of the landmarks of English history. Erasmus joined the founder and the first high master, Colet and Lily, in composing the schoolbooks to be used in it. He had already written, in More's house at Chelsea, where pure religion reigned alongside of high culture, the Encomium Moriae, in which all his immense gifts of eloquence and wit were lavished on the cause of humanism and the larger cause of humanity. That war was at once a sin, a scandal, and a folly was one of the central doctrines of the group of eminent Englishmen with whom he was now associated. It was a doctrine held by them with some ambiguity and in varying degrees. In the Utopia (1516) More condemns wars of aggression, while taking the common view as to wars of so-called self-defence. In 1513, when Henry, swept into the seductive scheme for a partition of France by a European confederacy, was preparing for the first of his many useless and inglorious continental campaigns, Colet spoke out more freely. He preached before the court against war itself as barbarous and unchristian, and did not spare either kings or popes who dealt otherwise. Henry was disturbed; he sent for Colet, and pressed him hard on the point whether he meant that all wars were unjustifiable. Colet was in advance of his age, but not so far in advance of it as this. He gave some kind of answer which satisfied the king. The preparations for war went forward; the Battle of Spurs plunged the court and all the nation into the intoxication of victory; while at Flodden-edge, in the same autumn, the ancestral allies of France sustained the most crushing defeat recorded in Scottish history. When both sides in a war have invoked God's favour, the successful side is ready enough to believe that its prayers have been answered and its action accepted by God.

Erasmus was now reader in Greek and professor of divinity at Cambridge; but Cambridge was far away from the centre of European thought and of literary activities. He left England before the end of the year for Basel, where the greater part of his life thenceforth was passed. Froben had made Basel the chief literary centre of production for the whole of Europe. Through Froben's printing-presses Erasmus could reach a wider audience than was allowed him at any court, however favourable to pure religion and the new learning. It was at this juncture that he made an eloquent and far-reaching appeal, on a matter which lay very near his heart, to the conscience of Christendom.

The Adagia, that vast work which was, at least to his own generation, Erasmus's foremost title to fame, has long ago passed into the rank of those monuments of literature "dont la reputation s'affermira toujours parcequ'on ne les lit guère." So far as Erasmus is more than a name for most modern readers, it is on slighter and more popular works that any direct knowledge of him is grounded on the Colloquies, which only ceased to be a schoolbook within living memory, on the Praise of Folly, and on selections from the enormous masses of his letters. An Oxford scholar of the last generation, whose profound knowledge of humanistic literature was accompanied by a gift of terse and pointed expression, describes the Adagia in a single sentence, as "a manual of the wit and wisdom of the ancient world for the use of the modern, enlivened by commentary in Erasmus's finest vein." In its first form, the Adagiorum Collectanea, it was published by him at Paris in 1500, just after his return from England. In the author's epistle dedicatory to Mountjoy he ascribes to him and to Richard Charnock, the prior of Saint Mary's College in Oxford, the inspiration of the work. It consists of a series of between eight and nine hundred comments in brief essays, each suggested by some terse or proverbial phrase from an ancient Latin author. The work gave full scope for the display, not only of the immense treasures of his learning, but of those other qualities, the combination of which raised their author far above all other contemporary writers, his keen wit, his copiousness and facility, his complete control of Latin as a living language. It met with an enthusiastic reception, and placed him at once at the head of European men of letters. Edition after edition poured from the press. It was ten times reissued at Paris within a generation. Eleven editions were published at Strasburg between 1509 and 1521. Within the same years it was reprinted at Erfurt, The Hague, Cologne, Mayence, Leyden, and elsewhere. The Rhine valley was the great nursery of letters north of the Alps, and along the Rhine from source to sea the book spread and was multiplied.

This success induced Erasmus to enlarge and complete his labours. The Adagiorum Chiliades, the title of the work in its new form, was part of the work of his residence in Italy in the years 1506-9, and was published at Venice by Aldus in September, 1508. The enlarged collection, to all intents and purposes a new work, consists of no less than three thousand two hundred and sixty heads. In a preface, Erasmus speaks slightingly of the Adagiorum Collectanea, with that affectation from which few authors are free, as a little collection carelessly made. "Some people got hold of it," he adds, (and here the affectation becomes absolute untruth,) "and had it printed very incorrectly." In the new work, however, much of the old disappears, much more is partially or wholly recast; and such of the old matter as is retained is dispersed at random among the new. In the Collectanea the commentaries had all been brief: here many are expanded into substantial treatises covering four or five pages of closely printed folio.

The Aldine edition had been reprinted at Basel by Froben in 1513. Shortly afterwards Erasmus himself took up his permanent residence there. Under his immediate supervision there presently appeared what was to all intents and purposes the definitive edition of 1515. It is a book of nearly seven hundred folio pages, and contains, besides the introductory matter, three thousand four hundred and eleven headings. In his preface Erasmus gives some details with regard to its composition. Of the original Paris work he now says, no doubt with truth, that it was undertaken by him hastily and without enough method. When preparing the Venice edition he had better realized the magnitude of the enterprise, and was better fitted for it by reading and learning, more especially by the mass of Greek manuscripts, and of newly printed Greek first editions, to which he had access at Venice and in other parts of Italy. In England also, owing very largely to the kindness of Archbishop Warham, more leisure and an ampler library had been available.

Among several important additions made in the edition of 1515, this essay, the text of which is the proverbial phrase "Dulce bellum inexpertis," is at once the longest and the most remarkable. The adage itself, with a few lines of commentary, had indeed been in the original collection; but the treatise, in itself a substantial work, now appeared for the first time. It occupied a conspicuous place as the first heading in the fourth Chiliad of the complete work; and it was at once singled out from the rest as of special note and profound import. Froben was soon called upon for a separate edition. This appeared in April, 1517, in a quarto of twenty pages. This little book, the Bellum Erasmi as it was called for the sake of brevity, ran like wildfire from reader to reader. Half the scholarly presses of Europe were soon employed in reprinting it. Within ten years it had been reissued at Louvain, twice at Strasburg, twice at Mayence, at Leipsic, twice at Paris, twice at Cologne, at Antwerp, and at Venice. German translations of it were published at Basel and at Strasburg in 1519 and 1520. It soon made its way to England, and the translation here utilized was issued by Berthelet, the king's printer, in the winter of 1533-4.

Whether the translation be by Richard Taverner, the translator and editor, a few years later, of an epitome or selection of the Chiliades, or by some other hand, there are no direct means of ascertaining; nor except for purposes of curiosity is the question an important one. The version wholly lacks distinction. It is a work of adequate scholarship but of no independent literary merit. English prose was then hardly formed. The revival of letters had reached the country, but for political and social reasons which are readily to be found in any handbook of English history, it had found a soil, fertile indeed, but not yet broken up. Since Chaucer, English poetry had practically stood still, and except where poetry has cleared the way, prose does not in ordinary circumstances advance. A few adventurers in setting forth had appeared. More's Utopia, one of the earliest of English prose classics, is a classic in virtue of its style as well as of its matter. Berners's translation of Froissart, published in 1523, was the first and one of the finest of that magnificent series of translations which from this time onwards for about a century were produced in an almost continuous stream, and through which the secret of prose was slowly wrung from older and more accomplished languages. Latimer, about the same time, showed his countrymen how a vernacular prose, flexible, well knit, and nervous, might be written without its lines being traced on any ancient or foreign model. Coverdale, the greatest master of English prose whom the century produced, whose name has just missed the immortality that is secure for his work, must have substantially completed that magnificent version of the Bible which appeared in 1535, and to which the authorized version of the seventeenth century owes all that one work of genius can owe to another. It is not with these great men that the translator of this treatise can be compared. But he wrought, after his measure, on the same structure as they.

Desiderius Erasmus

It is then to the original Latin, not to this rude and stammering version, that scholars must turn now, as still more certainly they turned then, for the mind of Erasmus; for with him, even more eminently than with other authors, the style is the man, and his Latin is the substance, not merely the dress, of his thought. When he wrote it he was about forty-eight years of age. He was still in the fullness of his power. If he was often crippled by delicate health, that was no more than he had habitually been from boyhood. In this treatise we come very near the real man, with his strange mixture of liberalism and orthodoxy, of clear-sighted courage and a delicacy which nearly always might be mistaken for timidity.

His text is that (in the translator's words) "nothing is either more wicked or more wretched, nothing doth worse become a man (I will not say a Christian man) than war." War was shocking to Erasmus alike on every side of his remarkably complex and sensitive nature. It was impious; it was inhuman; it was ugly; it was in every sense of the word barbarous, to one who before all things and in the full sense of the word was civilized and a lover of civilization. All these varied aspects of the case, seen by others singly and partially, were to him facets of one truth, rays of one light. His argument circles and flickers among them, hardly pausing to enforce one before passing insensibly to another. In the splendid vindication of the nature of man with which the treatise opens, the tone is rather that of Cicero than of the New Testament. The majesty of man resides above all in his capacity to "behold the very pure strength and nature of things;" in essence he is no fallen and corrupt creature, but a piece of workmanship such as Shakespeare describes him through the mouth of Hamlet. He was shaped to this heroic mould "by Nature, or rather god," so the Tudor translation reads, and the use of capital letters, though only a freak of the printer, brings out with a singular suggestiveness the latent pantheism which underlies the thought of all the humanists. To this wonderful creature strife and warfare are naturally repugnant. Not only is his frame "weak and tender," but he is "born to love and amity." His chief end, the object to which all his highest and most distinctively human powers are directed, is coöperant labour in the pursuit of knowledge. War comes out of ignorance, and into ignorance it leads; of war comes contempt of virtue and of godly living. In the age of Machiavelli the word "virtue" had a double and sinister meaning; but here it is taken in its nobler sense. Yet, the argument continues, for "virtue," even in the Florentine statesman's sense, war gives but little room. It is waged mainly for "vain titles or childish wrath;" it does not foster, in those responsible for it, any one of the nobler excellences. The argument throughout this part of the treatise is, both in its substance and in its ornament, wholly apart from the dogmas of religion. The furies of war are described as rising out of a very pagan hell. The apostrophe of Nature to mankind immediately suggests the spirit as well as the language of Lucretius. Erasmus had clearly been reading the De Rerum Natura, and borrows some of his finest touches from that miraculous description of the growth of civilization in the fifth book, which is one of the noblest contributions of antiquity towards a real conception of the nature of the world and of man. The progressive degeneration of morality, because, as its scope becomes higher, practice falls further and further short of it, is insisted upon by both these great thinkers in much the same spirit and with much the same illustrations. The rise of empires, "of which there was never none yet in any nation, but it was gotten with the great shedding of man's blood," is seen by both in the same light. But Erasmus passes on to the more expressly religious aspect of the whole matter in the great double climax with which he crowns his argument, the wickedness of a Christian fighting against another man, the horror of a Christian fighting against another Christian. "Yea, and with a thing so devilish," he breaks out in a mingling of intense scorn and profound pity, "we mingle Christ."

From this passionate appeal he passes to the praises of peace. Why should men add the horrors of war to all the other miseries and dangers of life? Why should one man's gain be sought only through another's loss? All victories in war are Cadmean; not only from their cost in blood and treasure, but because we are in very truth "the members of one body," "redeemed with Christ's blood." Such was the clear, unmistakable teaching of our Lord himself, such of his apostles. But the doctrine of Christ has been "plied to worldly opinion." Worldly men, philosophers following "the sophistries of Aristotle," worst of all, divines and theologians themselves, have corrupted the Gospel to the heathenish doctrine that "every man must first provide for himself." The very words of Scripture are wrested to this abuse. Self-defence is held to excuse any violence. "Peter fought," they say, "in the garden,"--yes, and that same night he denied his Master! "But punishment of wrong is a divine ordinance." In war the punishment falls on the innocent. "But the law of nature bids us repel violence by violence." What is the law of Christ? "But may not a prince go to war justly for his right?" Did any war ever lack a title? "But what of wars against the Turk?" Such wars are of Turk against Turk; let us overcome evil with good, let us spread the Gospel by doing what the Gospel commands: did Christ say, Hate them that hate you?

Then, with the tact of an accomplished orator, he lets the tension relax, and drops to a lower tone. Even apart from all that has been urged, even if war were ever justifiable, think of the price that has to be paid for it. On this ground alone an unjust peace is far preferable to a just war. (These had been the very words of Colet to the king of England.) Men go to war under fine pretexts, but really to get riches, to satisfy hatred, or to win the poor glory of destroying. The hatred is but exasperated; the glory is won

9

by and for the dregs of mankind; the riches are in the most prosperous event swallowed up ten times over. Yet if it be impossible but war should be, if there may be sometimes a "colour of equity" in it, and if the tyrant's plea, necessity, be ever well-founded, at least, so Erasmus ends, let it be conducted mercifully. Let us live in fervent desire of the peace that we may not fully attain. Let princes restrain their peoples; let churchmen above all be peacemakers. So the treatise passes to its conclusion with that eulogy of the Medicean pope already mentioned, which perhaps was not wholly undeserved. To the modern world the name of Leo X has come down marked with a note of censure or even of ignominy. It is fair to remember that it did not bear quite the same aspect to its contemporaries, nor to the ages which immediately followed. Under Rodrigo Borgia it might well seem to others than to the Florentine mystic that antichrist was enthroned, and Satan let loose upon earth. The eight years of Leo's pontificate (1513-21) were at least a period of outward splendour and of a refinement hitherto unknown. The corruption, half veiled by that refinement and splendour, was deep and mortal, but the collapse did not come till later. By comparison with the disastrous reign of Clement VII, his bastard cousin, that of Giovanni de' Medici seemed a last gleam of light before blackness descended on the world. Even the licence of a dissolute age was contrasted to its favour with the gloom, "tristitia," that settled down over Europe with the great Catholic reaction. The age of Leo X has descended to history as the age of Bembo, Sannazaro, Lascaris, of the Stanze of the Vatican, of Raphael's Sistine Madonna and Titian's Assumption; of the conquest of Mexico and the circumnavigation of Magellan; of Magdalen Tower and King's College Chapel. It was an interval of comparative peace before a long epoch of wars more cruel and more devastating than any within the memory of men. The general European conflagration did not break out until ten years after Erasmus's death; though it had then long been foreseen as inevitable. But he lived to see the conquest of Rhodes by Soliman, the sack of Rome, the breach between England and the papacy, the ill-omened marriage of Catherine de' Medici to the heir of the French throne. Humanism had done all that it could, and failed. In the sanguinary era of one hundred years between the outbreak of the civil war in the Empire and the Peace of Westphalia, the Renaissance followed the Middle Ages to the grave, and the modern world was born.

The mere fact of this treatise having been translated into English and published by the king's printer shows, in an age when the literary product of England was as yet scanty, that it had some vogue and exercised some influence. But only a few copies of the work are known to exist; and it was never reprinted. It was not until nearly three centuries later, amid the throes of an European revolution equally vast, that the work was again presented in an English dress. Vicesimus Knox, a whig essayist, compiler, and publicist of some reputation at the time, was the author of a book which was published anonymously in 1794 and found some readers in a year filled with great events in both the history and the literature of England. It was entitled "Anti-Polemus: or the Plea of Reason, Religion, and Humanity against War: a Fragment translated from Erasmus and addressed to Aggressors." That was the year when the final breach took place in the whig party, and when Pitt initiated his brief and ill-fated policy of conciliation in Ireland. It was also the year of two works of enormous influence over thought, Paley's Evidences and Paine's Age of Reason. Among these great movements Knox's work had but little chance of appealing to a wide audience. "Sed quid ad nos?" the bitter motto on the title-page, probably expressed the feelings with which it was generally regarded. A version of the treatise against war, made from the Latin text of the Adagia with some omissions, is the main substance of the volume; and Knox added a few extracts from other writings of Erasmus on the same subject. It does not appear to have been reprinted in England, except in a collected edition of Knox's works which may be found on the dustiest shelves of old-fashioned libraries, until, after the close of the Napoleonic wars, it was again published as a tract by the Society for the Promotion of Permanent and Universal Peace. Some half dozen impressions of this tract appeared at intervals up to the middle of the century; its publication passed into the hands of the Society of Friends, and the last issue of which any record can be found was made just before the outbreak of the Crimean war. But in 1813 an abridged edition was printed at New York, and was one of the books which influenced the great movement towards humanity then stirring in the young Republic.

At the present day, the reactionary wave which has overspread the world has led, both in England and America, to a new glorification of war. Peace is on the lips of governments and of individuals, but beneath the smooth surface the same passions, draped as they always have been under fine names, are a menace to progress and to the higher life of mankind. The increase of armaments, the glorification of the military life, the fanaticism which regards organized robbery and murder as a sacred imperial mission, are the fruits of a spirit which has fallen as far below the standard of humanism as it has left behind it the precepts of a still outwardly acknowledged religion. At such a time the noble pleading of Erasmus has more than a merely literary or antiquarian interest. For the appeal of humanism still is, as it was then, to the dignity of human nature itself.

J. W. Mackail

Desiderius Erasmus

DULCE BELLUM INEXPERTIS

It is both an elegant proverb, and among all others, by the writings of many excellent authors, full often and solemnly used, Dulce bellum inexpertis, that is to say, War is sweet to them that know it not. There be some things among mortal men's businesses, in the which how great danger and hurt there is, a man cannot perceive till he make a proof. The love and friendship of a great man is sweet to them that be not expert: he that hath had thereof experience, is afraid. It seemeth to be a gay and a glorious thing, to strut up and down among the nobles of the court, and to be occupied in the king's business; but old men, to whom that thing by long experience is well known, do gladly abstain themselves from such felicity. It seemeth a pleasant thing to be in love with a young damsel; but that is unto them that have not yet perceived how much grief and bitterness is in such love. So after this manner of fashion, this proverb may be applied to every business that is adjoined with great peril and with many evils: the which no man will take on hand, but he that is young and wanteth experience of things.

Aristotle, in his book of Rhetoric, showeth the cause why youth is more bold, and contrariwise old age more fearful: for unto young men lack of experience is cause of great boldness, and to the other, experience of many griefs engendereth fear and doubting. Then if there be anything in the world that should be taken in hand with fear and doubting, yea, that ought by all manner of means to be fled, to be withstood with prayer, and to be clean avoided, verily it is war; than which nothing is either more wicked, or more wretched, or that more farther destroyeth, or that never hand cleaveth sorer to, or doth more hurt, or is more horrible, and briefly to speak, nothing doth worse become a man (I will not say a Christian man) than war. And yet it is a wonder to speak of, how nowadays in every place, how lightly, and how for every trifling matter, it is taken in hand, how outrageously and barbarously it is gested and done, not only of heathen people, but also of Christian men; not only of secular men, but also of priests and bishops; not only of young men and of them that have no experience, but also of old men and of those that so often have had experience; not only of the common and movable vulgar people, but most specially of the princes, whose duty had been, by wisdom and reason, to set in a good order and to pacify the light and hasty movings of the foolish multitude. Nor there lack neither lawyers, nor yet divines, the which are ready with their firebrands to kindle these things so abominable, and they encourage them that else were cold, and they privily provoke those to it that were weary thereof. And by these means it is come to that pass that war is a thing now so well accepted, that men wonder at him that is not pleased therewith. It is so much approved, that it is counted a wicked thing (and I had almost said heresy) to reprove this one thing, the which as it is above all other things most mischievous, so it is most wretched. But how more justly should this be wondered at, what evil spirit, what pestilence, what mischief, and what madness put first in man's mind a thing so beyond measure beastly, that this most pleasant and reasonable creature Man, the which Nature hath brought forth to peace and benevolence, which one alone she hath brought forth to the help and succour of all other, should with so wild wilfulness, with so mad rages, run headlong one to destroy another? At the which thing he shall also much more marvel, whosoever would withdraw his mind from the opinions of the common people, and will turn it to behold the very pure strength and nature of things; and will apart behold with philosophical eyes the image of man on the one side, and the picture of war on the other side.

Then first of all if one would consider well but the behaviour and shape of man's body shall he not forthwith perceive that Nature, or rather God, hath shaped this creature, not to war, but to friendship, not to destruction, but to health, not to wrong, but to kindness and benevolence? For whereas Nature hath armed all other beasts with their own armour, as the violence of the bulls she hath armed with horns, the ramping lion with claws; to the boar she hath given the gnashing tusks; she hath armed the elephant with a long trump snout, besides his great huge body and hardness of the skin; she hath fenced the crocodile with a skin as hard as a plate; to the dolphin fish she hath given fins instead of a dart; the porcupine she defendeth with thorns; the ray and thornback with sharp prickles; to the cock she hath given strong spurs; some she fenceth with a shell, some with a hard hide, as it were thick leather, or bark of a tree; some she provideth to save by swiftness of flight, as doves; and to some she hath given venom instead of a weapon; to some she hath given a much horrible and ugly look, she hath given terrible eyes and grunting voice; and she hath also set among some of them continual dissension and debate--man alone she hath brought forth all naked, weak, tender, and without any armour, with most soft flesh and smooth skin. There is nothing at all in all his members that may seem to be ordained to war, or to any violence. I will not say at this time, that where all other beasts, anon as they are brought forth, they are able of themselves to get their food. Man alone cometh so forth, that a long season after he is born, he dependeth altogether on the help of others. He can neither speak nor go, nor yet take meat; he desireth help only by his infant crying: so that a man may, at the least way, by this conject, that this creature alone was born all to love and amity, which specially increaseth and is fast knit together by good turns done eftsoons of one to another. And for this cause Nature would, that a man should not so much thank her, for the gift of life, which she hath given unto him, as he should thank kindness and benevolence, whereby he might evidently understand himself, that he was altogether dedicate and bounden to the gods of graces, that is to say, to kindness, benevolence, and amity. And besides this Nature hath given unto man a countenance not terrible and loathly, as unto other brute beasts; but meek and demure, representing the very tokens of love and benevolence. She hath given him amiable eyes, and in them assured marks of the inward mind. She hath ordained him arms to clip and embrace. She hath given him the wit and understanding to kiss: whereby the very minds and hearts of men should be coupled together, even as though they touched each other. Unto man alone she hath given laughing, a token of good cheer and gladness. To man alone she hath given weeping tears, as it were a pledge or token of meekness and mercy. Yea, and she hath given him a voice not threatening and horrible, as unto other brute beasts, but amiable and pleasant. Nature not yet content with all this, she hath given unto man alone the commodity of speech and reasoning: the which things verily may specially both get and nourish benevolence, so that nothing at all should be done among men by violence.

She hath endued man with hatred of solitariness, and with love of company. She hath utterly sown in man the very seeds of benevolence. She hath so done, that the selfsame thing, that is most wholesome, should be most sweet and delectable. For what is more delectable than a friend? And again, what thing is more necessary? Moreover, if a man might lead all his life most profitably without any meddling with other men, yet nothing would seem pleasant without a fellow: except a man would cast off all humanity, and forsaking his own kind would become a beast.

Besides all this, Nature hath endued man with knowledge of liberal sciences and a fervent desire of knowledge: which thing as it doth most specially withdraw man's wit from all beastly wildness, so hath it a special grace to get and knit together love and friendship. For I dare boldly say, that neither affinity nor yet kindred doth bind the minds of men together with straiter and surer bands of amity, than doth the fellowship of them that be learned in good letters and honest studies. And above all this, Nature hath divided among men by a marvellous variety the gifts, as well of the soul as of the body, to the intent truly that every man might find in every singular person one thing or other, which they should either love or praise for the excellency thereof; or else greatly desire and make much of it, for the need and profit that cometh thereof. Finally she hath endowed man with a spark of a godly mind: so that though he see no reward, yet of his own courage he delighteth to do every man good: for unto God it is most proper and natural, by his benefit, to do everybody good. Else what meaneth it, that we rejoice and conceive in our minds no little pleasure when we perceive that any creature is by our means preserved.

Moreover God hath ordained man in this world, as it were the very image of himself, to the intent, that he, as it were a god on earth, should provide for the wealth of all creatures. And this thing the very brute beasts do also perceive, for we may see, that not only the tame beasts, but also the leopards, lions, and other more fierce and wild, when they be in any great jeopardy, they flee to man for succour. So man is, when all things fail, the last refuge to all manner of creatures. He is unto them all the very assured altar and sanctuary.

I have here painted out to you the image of man as well as I can. On the other side (if it like you) against the figure of Man, let us portray the fashion and shape of War.

Now, then, imagine in thy mind, that thou dost behold two hosts of barbarous people, of whom the look is fierce and cruel, and the voice horrible; the terrible and fearful rustling and glistering of their harness and weapons; the unlovely murmur of so huge a multitude; the eyes sternly menacing; the bloody blasts and terrible sounds of trumpets and clarions; the thundering of the guns, no less fearful than thunder indeed, but much more hurtful; the frenzied cry and clamour, the furious and mad running together, the outrageous slaughter, the cruel chances of them that flee and of those that are stricken down and slain, the heaps of slaughters, the fields overflowed with blood, the rivers dyed red with man's blood. And it chanceth oftentimes, that the brother fighteth with the brother, one kinsman with another, friend against friend; and in that common furious desire ofttimes one thrusteth his weapon quite through the body of another that never gave him so much as a foul word. Verily, this tragedy containeth so many mischiefs, that it would abhor any man's heart to speak thereof. I will let pass to speak of the hurts which are in comparison of the other but light and common, as the treading down and destroying of the corn all about, the burning of towns, the villages fired, the driving away of cattle, the ravishing of maidens, the old men led forth in captivity, the robbing of churches, and all things confounded and full of thefts, pillages, and violence. Neither I will not speak now of those things which are wont to follow the most happy and most just war of all.

The poor commons pillaged, the nobles overcharged; so many old men of their children bereaved, yea, and slain also in the slaughter of their children; so many old women destitute, whom sorrow more

Desiderius Erasmus

cruelly slayeth than the weapon itself; so many honest wives become widows, so many children fatherless, so many lamentable houses, so many rich men brought to extreme poverty. And what needeth it here to speak of the destruction of good manners, since there is no man but knoweth right well that the universal pestilence of all mischievous living proceedeth at once from war. Thereof cometh despising of virtue and godly living; thereof cometh, that the laws are neglected and not regarded; thereof cometh a prompt and a ready stomach, boldly to do every mischievous deed. Out of this fountain spring so huge great companies of thieves, robbers, sacrilegers, and murderers. And what is most grievous of all, this mischievous pestilence cannot keep herself within her bounds; but after it is begun in some one corner, it doth not only (as a contagious disease) spread abroad and infect the countries near adjoining to it, but also it draweth into that common tumult and troublous business the countries that be very far off, either for need, or by reason of affinity, or else by occasion of some league made. Yea and moreover, one war springeth of another: of a dissembled war there cometh war indeed, and of a very small, a right great war hath risen. Nor it chanceth oftentimes none otherwise in these things than it is feigned of the monster, which lay in the lake or pond called Lerna.

For these causes, I trow, the old poets, the which most sagely perceived the power and nature of things, and with most meet feignings covertly shadowed the same, have left in writing, that war was sent out of hell: nor every one of the Furies was not meet and convenient to bring about this business, but the most pestilent and mischievous of them all was chosen out for the nonce, which hath a thousand names, and a thousand crafts to do hurt. She being armed with a thousand serpents, bloweth before her her fiendish trumpet. Pan with furious ruffling encumbereth every place. Bellona shaketh her furious flail. And then the wicked furiousness himself, when he hath undone all knots and broken all bonds, rusheth out with bloody mouth horrible to behold.

The grammarians perceived right well these things, of the which some will, that war have his name by contrary meaning of the word Bellum, that is to say fair, because it hath nothing good nor fair. Nor bellum, that is for to say war, is none otherwise called Bellum, that is to say fair, than the furies are called Eumenides, that is to say meek, because they are wilful and contrary to all meekness. And some grammarians think rather, that bellum, war, should be derived out of this word Belva, that is for to say, a brute beast: forasmuch as it belongeth to brute beasts, and not unto men, to run together, each to destroy each other. But it seemeth to me far to pass all wild and all brute beastliness, to fight together with weapons.

First, for there are many of the brute beasts, each in his kind, that agree and live in a gentle fashion together, and they go together in herds and flocks, and each helpeth to defend the other. Nor is it the nature of all wild beasts to fight, for some are harmless, as does and hares. But they that are the most fierce of all, as lions, wolves, and tigers, do not make war among themselves as we do. One dog eateth not another. The lions, though they be fierce and cruel, yet they fight not among themselves. One dragon is in peace with another. And there is agreement among poisonous serpents. But unto man there is no wild or cruel beast more hurtful than man.

Again, when the brute beasts fight, they fight with their own natural armour: we men, above nature, to the destruction of men, arm ourselves with armour, invented by craft of the devil. Nor the wild beasts are not cruel for every cause; but either when hunger maketh them fierce, or else when they perceive themselves to be hunted and pursued to the death, or else when they fear lest their younglings should take any harm or be stolen from them. But (O good Lord) for what trifling causes what tragedies of war do we stir up? For most vain titles, for childish wrath, for a wench, yea, and for causes much more scornful than these, we be inflamed to fight.

Moreover, when the brute beasts fight, then war is one for one, yea, and that is very short. And when the battle is sorest fought, yet is there not past one or two, that goeth away sore wounded. When was it ever heard that an hundred thousand brute beasts were slain at one time fighting and tearing one another: which thing men do full oft and in many places? And besides this, whereas some wild beasts have natural debate with some other that be of a contrary kind, so again there be some with which they lovingly agree in a sure amity. But man with man, and each with other, have among them continual war; nor is there league sure enough among any men. So that whatsoever it be, that hath gone out of kind, it hath gone out of kind into a worse fashion, than if Nature herself had engendered therein a malice at the beginning.

Will ye see how beastly, how foul, and how unworthy a thing war is for man? Did ye never behold a lion let loose unto a bear? What gapings, what roarings, what grisly gnashing, what tearing of their flesh, is there? He trembleth that beholdeth them, yea, though he stand sure and safe enough from them. But how much more grisly a sight is it, how much more outrageous and cruel, to behold man to fight with man, arrayed with so much armour, and with so many weapons? I beseech you, who would believe that they were men, if it were not because war is a thing so much in custom that no man marvelleth at it? Their eyes glow like fire, their faces be pale, their marching forth is like men in a fury, their voice screeching and grunting, their cry and frenzied clamour; all is iron, their harness and weapons jingling and clattering, and the guns thundering. It might have been better suffered, if man, for lack of meat and drink, should have fought with man, to the intent he might devour his flesh and drink his blood: albeit, it is come also now to that pass, that some there be that do it more of hatred than either for hunger or for thirst. But now this same thing is done more cruelly, with weapons envenomed, and with devilish engines. So that nowhere may be perceived any token of man. Trow ye that Nature could here know it was the same thing, that she sometime had wrought with her own hands? And if any man would inform her, that it were man that she beheld in such array, might she not well, with great wondering, say these words?

"What new manner of pageant is this that I behold? What devil of hell hath brought us forth this monster. There be some that call me a stepmother, because that among so great heaps of things of my making I have brought forth some venomous things (and yet have I ordained the selfsame venomous things for man's behoof); and because I have made some beasts very fierce and perilous: and yet is there no beast so wild nor so perilous, but that by craft and diligence he may be made tame and gentle. By man's diligent labour the lions have been made tame, the dragons meek, and the bears obedient. But what is this, that worse is than any stepmother, which hath brought us forth this new unreasonable brute beast, the pestilence and mischief of all this world? One beast alone I brought forth wholly dedicate to be benevolent, pleasant, friendly, and wholesome to all other. What hath chanced, that this creature is changed into such a brute beast? I perceive nothing of the creature man, which I myself made. What evil spirit hath thus defiled my work? What witch hath bewitched the mind of man, and transformed it into such brutishness? What sorceress hath thus turned him out of his kindly shape? I command and would that the wretched creature should behold himself in a glass. But, alas, what shall the eyes see, where the mind is away? Yet behold thyself (if thou canst), thou furious warrior, and see if thou mayst by any means recover thyself again. From whence hast thou that threatening crest upon thy head? From whence hast thou that shining helmet? From whence are those iron horns? Whence cometh it, that thine elbows are so sharp and piked? Where hadst thou those scales? Where hadst thou those brazen teeth? Of whence are those hard plates? Whence are those deadly weapons? From whence cometh to thee this voice more horrible than of a wild beast? What a look and countenance hast thou more terrible than of a brute beast? Where hast thou gotten this thunder and lightning, both more fearful and hurtful than is the very thunder and lightning itself? I formed thee a goodly creature; what came into thy mind, that thou wouldst thus transform thyself into so cruel and so beastly fashion, that there is no brute beast so unreasonable in comparison unto man?"

These words, and many other such like, I suppose, the Dame Nature, the worker of all things, would say. Then since man is such as is showed before that he is, and that war is such a thing, like as too oft we have felt and known, it seemeth to me no small wonder, what ill spirit, what disease, or what mishap, first put into man's mind, that he would bathe his mortal weapon in the blood of man. It must needs be, that men mounted up to so great madness by divers degrees. For there was never man yet (as Juvenal saith) that was suddenly most graceless of all. And always things the worst have crept in among men's manners of living, under the shadow and shape of goodness. For some time those men that were in the beginning of the world led their lives in woods; they went naked, they had no walled towns, nor houses to put their heads in: it happened otherwhile that they were sore grieved and destroyed with wild beasts. Wherefore with them first of all, men made war, and he was esteemed a mighty strong man, and a captain, that could best defend mankind from the violence of wild beasts. Yea, and it seemed to them a thing most equable to strangle the stranglers, and to slay the slayers, namely, when the wild beast, not provoked by us for any hurt to them done, would wilfully set upon us. And so by reason that this was counted a thing most worthy of praise (for hereof it rose that Hercules was made a god), the lusty-stomached young men began all about to hunt and chase the wild beasts, and as a token of their valiant victory the skins of such beasts as they slew were set up in such places as the people might behold them. Besides this they were not contented to slay the wild beasts, but they used to wear their skins to keep them from the cold in winter. These were the first slaughters that men used: these were their spoils and robberies. After this, they went so farforth, that they were bold to do a thing which Pythagoras thought to be very wicked; and it might seem to us also a thing monstrous, if custom were not, which hath so great strength in every place: that by custom it was reputed in some countries a much charitable deed if a man would, when his father was very old, first sore beat him, and after thrust him headlong into a pit, and so bereave him of his life, by whom it chanced him to have the gift of life. It was counted a holy thing for a man to feed on the flesh of his own kinsmen and friends. They thought it a goodly thing, that a virgin should be made common to the people in the temple of Venus. And many other things, more abominable than these: of which if a man should now but only speak, every man would abhor to hear him. Surely there is nothing so ungracious, nor nothing so cruel, but men will hold therewith, if it be once approved by custom. Then will ye hear, what a deed they durst at the last do? They were not abashed to eat the carcases of the wild beasts that were slain, to tear the unsavoury flesh with their teeth, to drink the blood, to suck out the matter of them, and (as Ovid saith) to hide the beasts' bowels within their own. And although at that time it seemed to be an outrageous deed unto them that were of a more mild and gentle courage: yet was it generally allowed, and all by reason of custom and commodity. Yet were they not so content. For they went from the slaying of noisome wild beasts, to kill the harmless beasts, and such as did no hurt at all. They waxed cruel everywhere upon the poor sheep, a beast without fraud or guile. They slew the hare, for none other offence, but because he was a good fat dish of meat to feed upon. Nor they forbare not to kill the tame ox, which had a long season, with his sore labour, nourished the unkind household. They spared no kind of beasts, of fowls, nor of fishes. Yea, and the tyranny of gluttony went so farforth that there was no beast anywhere that could be sure from the cruelty of man. Yea, and custom persuaded this also, that it seemed no cruelty at all to slay any manner of beast, whatsoever it was, so they abstained from manslaughter. Now peradventure it lieth in our power to keep out vices, that they enter not upon the manners of men, in like manner as it lieth in our power to keep out the sea, that it break not in upon us; but when the sea is once broken in, it passeth our power to restrain it within any bounds. So either of them both once let in, they will not be ruled, as we would, but run forth headlong whithersoever their own rage carrieth them. And so after that men had been exercised with such beginnings to slaughter, wrath anon enticed man to set upon man, either with staff, or with stone, or else with his fist. For as yet, I think they used no other weapons. And now had they learned by the killing of beasts, that man also might soon and easily be slain with little labour. But this cruelty remained betwixt singular persons, so that yet there was no great number of men that fought together, but as it chanced one man against another. And besides this, there was no small colour of equity, if a man slew his enemy; yea, and shortly after, it was a great praise to a man to slay a violent and a mischievous man, and to rid him out of the world, such devilish and cruel caitiffs, as men say Cacus and Busiris were. For we see plainly, that for such causes, Hercules was greatly praised. And in process of time, many assembled to take part together, either as affinity, or as neighbourhood, or kindred bound them. And what is now robbery was then war. And they fought then with stones, or with stakes, a little burned at the ends. A little river, a rock, or such other like thing, chancing to be between them, made an end of their battle.

In the mean season, while fierceness by use increaseth, while wrath is grown great, and ambition hot and vehement, by ingenious craft they arm their furious violence. They devise harness, such as it is, to fence them with. They invent weapons to destroy their enemies with. Thus now by few and few, now with greater company, and now armed they begin to fight. Nor to this manifest madness they forget not to give honour. For they call it Bellum, that is to say, a fair thing; yea, and they repute it a virtuous deed, if a man, with the jeopardy of his own life, manly resist and defend from the violence of his enemies, his wife, children, beasts, and household. And by little and little, malice grew so great, with the high esteeming of other things, that one city began to send defiance and make war to another, country against country, and realm against realm. And though the thing of itself was then most cruel, yet all this while there remained in them certain tokens, whereby they might be known for men: for such goods as by violence were taken away were asked and required again by an herald at arms; the gods were called to witness; yea, and when they were ranged in battle, they would reason the matter ere they fought. And in the battle they used but homely weapons, nor they used neither guile nor deceit, but only strength. It was not lawful for a man to strike his enemy till the sign of battle was given; nor was it not lawful to fight after the sounding of the retreat. And for conclusion, they fought more to show their manliness and for praise, than they coveted to slay. Nor all this while they armed them not, but against strangers, the which they called hostes, as they had been hospites, their guests. Of this rose empires, of the which there was never none yet in any nation, but it was gotten with the great shedding of man's blood. And since that time there hath followed continual course of war, while one eftsoons laboureth to put another out of his empire, and to set himself in. After all this, when the empires came once into their hands that were most ungracious of all other, they made war upon whosoever pleased them; nor were they not in greatest peril and danger of war that had most deserved to be punished, but they that by fortune had gotten great riches. And now they made not war to get praise and fame, but to get the vile muck of the world, or else some other thing far worse than that.

I think not the contrary, but that the great, wise man Pythagoras meant these things when he by a proper device of philosophy frightened the unlearned multitude of people from the slaying of silly beasts. For he perceived, it should at length come to pass, that he which (by no injury provoked) was accustomed to spill the blood of a harmless beast, would in his anger, being provoked by injury, not fear to slay a man.

War, what other thing else is it than a common manslaughter of many men together, and a robbery, the which, the farther it sprawleth abroad, the more mischievous it is? But many gross gentlemen nowadays laugh merrily at these things, as though they were the dreams and dotings of schoolmen, the which, saving the shape, have no point of manhood, yet seem they in their own conceit to be gods. And yet of those beginnings, we see we be run so far in madness, that we do naught else all our life-days. We war continually, city with city, prince with prince, people with people, yea, and (it that the heathen people confess to be a wicked thing) cousin with cousin, alliance with alliance, brother with brother, the son with the father, yea, and that I esteem more cruel than all these things, a Christian man against another man; and yet furthermore, I will say that I am very loath to do, which is a thing most cruel of all, one Christian man with another Christian man. Oh, blindness of man's mind! at those things no man marvelleth, no man abhorreth them. There be some that rejoice at them, and praise them above the moon: and the thing which is more than devilish, they call a holy thing. Old men, crooked for age, make war, priests make war, monks go forth to war; yea, and with a thing so devilish we mingle Christ. The battles ranged, they encounter the one the other, bearing before them the sign of the Cross, which thing alone might at the leastwise admonish us by what means it should become Christian men to overcome.

But we run headlong each to destroy other, even from that heavenly sacrifice of the altar, whereby is represented that perfect and ineffable knitting together of all Christian men. And of so wicked a thing, we make Christ both author and witness. Where is the kingdom of the devil, if it be not in war? Why draw we Christ into war, with whom a brothel-house agreeth more than war? Saint Paul disdaineth, that there should be any so great discord among Christian men, that they should need any judge to discuss the matter between them. What if he should come and behold us now through all the world, warring for every light and trifling cause, striving more cruelly than ever did any heathen people, and more cruelly than any barbarous people? Yea, and ye shall see it done by the authority, exhortations, and furtherings of those that represent Christ, the prince of peace and very bishop that all things knitteth together by peace and of those that salute the people with good luck of peace. Nor is it not unknown to me what these unlearned people say (a good while since) against me in this matter, whose winnings arise of the common evils. They say thus: We make war against our wills: for we be constrained by the ungracious deeds of other. We make war but for our right. And if there come any hurt thereof, thank them that be causers of it. But let these men hold their tongues awhile, and I shall after, in place convenient, avoid all their cavillations, and pluck off that false visor wherewith we hide all our malice.

But first as I have above compared man with war, that is to say, the creature most demure with a thing most outrageous, to the intent that cruelty might the better be perceived: so will I compare war and peace together, the thing most wretched, and most mischievous, with the best and most wealthy thing that is. And so at last shall appear, how great madness it is, with so great tumult, with so great labours, with such intolerable expenses, with so many calamities, affectionately to desire war: whereas agreement might be bought with a far less price.

First of all, what in all this world is more sweet or better than amity or love? Truly nothing. And I pray you, what other thing is peace than amity and love among men, like as war on the other side is naught else but dissension and debate of many men together? And surely the property of good things is such, that the broader they be spread, the more profit and commodity cometh of them. Farther, if the love of one singular person with another be so sweet and delectable, how great should the felicity be if realm with realm, and nation with nation, were coupled together, with the band of amity and love? On the other side, the nature of evil things is such, that the farther they sprawl abroad, the more worthy they are to be called evil, as they be indeed. Then if it be a wretched thing, if it be an ungracious thing, that one man armed should fight with another, how much more miserable, how much more mischievous is it, that the selfsame thing should be done with so many thousands together? By love and peace the small things increase and wax great, by discord and debate the great things decay and come to naught. Peace is the mother and nurse of all good things. War suddenly and at once overthroweth, destroyeth, and utterly fordoeth everything that is pleasant and fair, and bringeth in among men a monster of all mischievous things.

In the time of peace (none otherwise than as if the lusty springtime should show and shine in men's businesses) the fields are tilled, the gardens and orchards freshly flourish, the beasts pasture merrily; gay manours in the country are edified, the towns are builded, where as need is reparations are done, the buildings are heightened and augmented, riches increase, pleasures are nourished, the laws are executed, the common wealth flourisheth, religion is fervent, right reigneth, gentleness is used, craftsmen are busily exercised, the poor men's gain is more plentiful, the wealthiness of the rich men is more gay and goodly, the studies of most honest learnings flourish, youth is well taught, the aged folks have quiet and rest, maidens are luckily married, mothers are praised for bringing forth of children like to their progenitors, the good men prosper and do well, and the evil men do less offence.

But as soon as the cruel tempest of war cometh on us, good Lord, how great a flood of mischiefs occupieth, overfloweth, and drowneth all together. The fair herds of beasts are driven away, the goodly corn is trodden down and destroyed, the good husbandmen are slain, the villages are burned up, the most wealthy cities, that have flourished so many winters, with that one storm are overthrown, destroyed, and brought to naught: so much readier and prompter men are to do hurt than good. The good citizens are robbed and spoiled of their goods by cursed thieves and murderers. Every place is full of fear, of wailing, complaining, and lamenting. The craftsmen stand idle; the poor men must either die for hunger, or fall to stealing. The rich men either stand and sorrow for their goods, that be plucked and snatched from them, or else they stand in great doubt to lose such goods as they have left them: so that they be on every side woebegone. The maidens, either they be not married at all, or else if they be married, their marriages are sorrowful and lamentable. Wives, being destitute of their husbands, lie at home without any fruit of children, the laws are laid aside, gentleness is laughed to scorn, right is clean exiled, religion is set at naught, hallowed and unhallowed things all are one, youth is corrupted with all manner of vices, the old folk wail and weep, and wish themselves out of the world, there is no honour given unto the study of good letters. Finally, there is no tongue can tell the harm and mischief that we feel in war.

Perchance war might be the better suffered, if it made us but only wretched and needy; but it maketh us ungracious, and also full of unhappiness. And I think Peace likewise should be much made of, if it were but only because it maketh us more wealthy and better in our living. Alas, there be too many already, yea, and more than too many mischiefs and evils, with the which the wretched life of man (whether he will or no) is continually vexed, tormented, and utterly consumed.

It is near hand two thousand years since the physicians had knowledge of three hundred divers notable sicknesses by name, besides other small sicknesses and new, as daily spring among us, and besides age also, which is of itself a sickness inevitable.

We read that in one place whole cities have been destroyed with earthquakes. We read, also, that in another place there have been cities altogether burnt with lightning; how in another place whole regions have been swallowed up with opening of the earth, towns by undermining have fallen to the ground; so that I need not here to remember what a great multitude of men are daily destroyed by divers chances, which be not regarded because they happen so often: as sudden breaking out of the sea and of great floods, falling down of hills and houses, poison, wild beasts, meat, drink, and sleep. One hath been strangled with drinking of a hair in a draught of milk, another hath been choked with a little grapestone, another with a fishbone sticking in his throat. There hath been, that sudden joy hath killed out of hand: for it is less wonder of them that die for vehement sorrow. Besides all this, what mortal pestilence see we in every place. There is no part of the world, that is not subject to peril and danger of man's life, which life of itself also is most fugitive. So manifold mischances and evils assail man on every side that not without cause Homer did say: Man was the most wretched of all creatures living.

But forasmuch these mischances cannot lightly be eschewed, nor they happen not through our fault, they make us but only wretched, and not ungracious withal. What pleasure is it then for them that be subject already to so many miserable chances, willingly to seek and procure themselves another mischief more than they had before, as though they yet wanted misery? Yea, they procure not a light evil, but such an evil that is worse than all the others, so mischievous, that it alone passeth all the others; so abundant, that in itself alone is comprehended all ungraciousness; so pestilent, that it maketh us all alike wicked as wretched, it maketh us full of all misery, and yet not worthy to be pitied.

Now go farther, and with all these things consider, that the commodities of Peace spread themselves most far and wide, and pertain unto many men. In war if there happen anything luckily (but, O good Lord, what may we say happeneth well and luckily in war?), it pertaineth to very few, and to them that are unworthy to have it. The prosperity of one is the destruction of another. The enriching of one is the spoil and robbing of another. The triumph of one is the lamentable mourning of another, so that as the infelicity is bitter and sharp, the felicity is cruel and bloody. Howbeit otherwhile both parties wept according to the proverb, Victoria Cadmaea, Cadmus victorie, where both parties repented. And I wot not whether it came ever so happily to pass in war, that he that had victory did not repent him of his enterprise, if he were a good man.

Then seeing Peace is the thing above all other most best and most pleasant, and, contrariwise, war the thing most ungracious and wretched of all other, shall we think those men to be in their right minds, the which when they may obtain Peace with little business and labour will rather procure war with so great labour and most difficulty?

First of all consider, how loathly a thing the rumour of war is, when it is first spoken of. Then how envious a thing it is unto a prince, while with often tithes and taxes he pillageth his subjects. What a business hath he to make and entertain friends to help him? what a business to procure bands of strangers and to hire soldiers?

What expenses and labours must he make in setting forth his navy of ships, in building and repairing of castles and fortresses, in preparing and apparelling of his tents and pavilions, in framing, making, and carrying of engines, guns, armour, weapons, baggage, carts, and victual? What great labour is spent in making of bulwarks, in casting of ditches, in digging of mines, in keeping of watches, in keeping of arrays, and in exercising of weapons? I pass over the fear they be in; I speak not of the imminent danger and peril that hangeth over their heads: for what thing in war is not to be feared? What is he that can reckon all the incommodious life that the most foolish soldiers suffer in the field? And for that worthy to endure worse, in that they will suffer it willingly. Their meat is so ill that an ox of Cyprus would be loath to eat it; they have but little sleep, nor yet that at their own pleasure. Their tents on every side are open on the wind. What, a tent? No, no; they must all the day long, be it hot or cold, wet or dry, stand in the open air, sleep on the bare ground, stand in their harness. They must suffer hunger, thirst, cold, heat, dust, showers; they must be obedient to their captains; sometimes they be clapped on the pate with a warder or a truncheon: so that there is no bondage so vile as the bondage of soldiers.

Against War and In Praise of Folly

Besides all this, at the sorrowful sign given to fight, they must run headlong to death: for either they must slay cruelly, or be slain wretchedly. So many sorrowful labours must they take in hand, that they may bring to pass that thing which is most wretched of all other. With so many great miseries we must first afflict and grieve our own self, that we may afflict and grieve other!

Now if we would call this matter to account, and justly reckon how much war will cost, and how much peace, surely we shall find that peace may be got and obtained with the tenth part of the cares, labours, griefs, perils, expenses, and spilling of blood, with which the war is procured. So great a company of men, to their extreme perils, ye lead out of the realm to overthrow and destroy some one town: and with the labour of the selfsame men, and without any peril at all, another town, much more noble and goodly, might be new edified and builded. But you say, you will hurt and grieve your enemy: so even that doing is against humanity. Nevertheless, this I would ye should consider, that ye cannot hurt and grieve your enemies, but ye must first greatly hurt your own people. And it seemeth a point of a madman, to enterprise where he is sure and certain of so great hurt and damage, and is uncertain which way the chance of war will turn.

But admit, that either foolishness, or wrath, or ambition, or covetousness, or outrageous cruelty, or else (which I think more like) the furies sent from hell, should ravish and draw the heathen people to this madness. Yet from whence cometh it into our minds, that one Christian man should draw his weapon to bathe it in another Christian man's blood? It is called parricide, if the one brother slay the other. And yet is a Christian man nearer joined to another than is one brother to another: except the bonds of nature be stronger than the bonds of Christ. What abominable thing, then, is it to see them almost continually fighting among themselves, the which are the inhabitants of one house the Church, which rejoice and say, that they all be the members of one body, and that have one head, which truly is Christ; they have all one Father in heaven; they are all taught and comforted by one Holy Spirit; they profess the religion of Christ all under one manner; they are all redeemed with Christ's blood; they are all newborn at the holy font; they use alike sacraments; they be all soldiers under one captain; they are all fed with one heavenly bread; they drink all of one spiritual cup; they have one common enemy the devil; finally, they be all called to one inheritance. Where be they so many sacraments of perfect concord? Where be the innumerable teachings of peace? There is one special precept, which Christ called his, that is, Charity. And what thing is so repugnant to charity as war? Christ saluted his disciples with the blessed luck of peace. Unto his disciples he gave nothing save peace, saving peace he left them nothing. In those holy prayers, he specially prayed the Father of heaven, that in like manner as he was one with the Father, so all his, that is to say, Christian men, should be one with him. Lo, here you may perceive a thing more than peace, more than amity, more than concord.

Solomon bare the figure of Christ: for Solomon in the Hebrew tongue signifieth peaceable or peaceful. Him God would have to build his temple. At the birth of Christ the angels proclaimed neither war nor triumphs, but peace they sang. And before his birth the prophet David prophesied thus of him: Et factus est in pace locus ejus, that is to say, His dwelling place is made in peace. Search all the whole life of Christ, and ye shall never find thing that breathes not of peace, that signifieth not amity, that savoureth not of charity. And because he perceived peace could not well be kept, except men would utterly despise all those things for which the world so greedily fighteth, he commanded that we should of him learn to be meek. He calleth them blessed and happy that setteth naught by riches, for those he calleth poor in spirit. Blessed be they that despise the pleasures of this world, the which he calleth mourners. And them blessed he calleth that patiently suffer themselves, to be put out of their possessions, knowing that here in this world they are but as outlaws; and the very true country and possession of godly creatures is in heaven. He calleth them blessed which, deserving well of all men, are wrongfully blamed and ill afflicted. He forbade that any man should resist evil. Briefly, as all his doctrine commandeth sufferance and love, so all his life teacheth nothing else but meekness. So he reigned, so he warred, so he overcame, so he triumphed.

Now the apostles, that had sucked into them the pure spirit of Christ, and were blessedly drunk with that new must of the Holy Ghost, preached nothing but meekness and peace. What do all the epistles of Paul sound in every place but peace, but long-suffering, but charity? What speaketh Saint John, what rehearseth he so oft, but love? What other thing did Peter? What other thing did all the true Christian writers? From whence then cometh all this tumult of wars amongst the children of peace? Think ye it a fable, that Christ calleth himself a vine tree, and his own the branches? Who did ever see one branch fight with another? Is it in vain that Paul so oft wrote, The Church to be none other thing, than one body compact together of divers members, cleaving to one head, Christ? Whoever saw the eye fight with the hand, or the belly with the foot? In this universal body, compact of all those unlike things, there is agreement. In the body of a beast, one member is in peace with another, and each member useth not the property thereto given for itself alone, but for the profit of all the other members. So that if there come any good to any one member alone, it helpeth all the whole body. And may the compaction or knitting of Nature do more in the body of a beast, that shortly must perish, than the coupling of the Holy Ghost in the mystical and immortal body of the Church? Do we to no purpose pray as taught by Christ:

Desiderius Erasmus

Good Lord, even as thy will is fulfilled in heaven, so let it be fulfilled in the earth? In that city of heaven is concord and peace most perfect. And Christ would have his Church to be none other than a heavenly people in earth, as near as might be after the manner of them that are in heaven, ever labouring and making haste to go thither, and always having their mind thereon.

Now go to, let us imagine, that there should come some new guest out of the lunar cities, where Empedocles dwelleth, or else out of the innumerable worlds, that Democritus fabricated, into this world, desiring to know what the inhabitants do here. And when he was instructed of everything, it should at last be told him that, besides all other, there is one creature marvellously mingled, of body like to brute beasts and of soul like unto God. And it should also be told him, that this creature is so noble, that though he be here an outlaw out of his own country, yet are all other beasts at his commandment, the which creature through his heavenly beginning inclineth alway to things heavenly and immortal. And that God eternal loved this creature so well, that whereas he could neither by the gifts of nature, nor by the strong reasons of philosophy attain unto that which he so fervently desired, he sent hither his only begotten son, to the intent to teach this creature a new kind of learning. Then as soon as this new guest had perceived well the whole manner of Christ's life and precepts, would desire to stand in some high place, from whence he might behold that which he had heard. And when he should see all other creatures soberly live according to their kind, and, being led by the laws and course of nature, desire nothing but even as Nature would; and should see this one special creature man given riotously to tavern haunting, to vile lucre, to buying and selling, chopping and changing, to brawling and fighting one with another, trow ye that he would not think that any of the other creatures were man, of whom he heard so much of before, rather than he that is indeed man? Then if he that had instructed him afore would show him which creature is man, now would he look about to see if he could spy the Christian flock and company, the which, following the ordinance of that heavenly teacher Christ, should exhibit to him a figure or shape of the evangelical city. Think ye he would not rather judge Christians to dwell in any other place than in those countries, wherein we see so great superfluity, riot, voluptuousness, pride, tyranny, discord, brawlings, fightings, wars, tumults, yea, and briefly to speak, a greater puddle of all those things that Christ reproveth than among Turks or Saracens? From whence, then, creepeth this pestilence in among Christian people? Doubtless this mischief also is come in by little and little, like as many more other be, ere men be aware of them. For truly every mischief creepeth by little and little upon the good manners of men, or else under the colour of goodness it is suddenly received.

So then first of all, learning and cunning crept in as a thing very meet to confound heretics, which defend their opinions with the doctrine of philosophers, poets, and orators. And surely at the beginning of our faith, Christian men did not learn those things; but such as peradventure had learned them, before they knew what Christ meant, they turned the thing that they had learned already, into good use.

Eloquence of tongue was at the beginning dissembled more than despised, but at length it was openly approved. After that, under colour of confounding heretics, came in an ambitious pleasure of brawling disputations, which hath brought into the Church of Christ no small mischief. At length the matter went so farforth that Aristotle was altogether received into the middle of divinity, and so received, that his authority is almost reputed holier than the authority of Christ. For if Christ spake anything that did little agree with our life, by interpretation of Aristotle it was lawful to make it serve their purpose. But if any do never so little repugn against the high divinity of Aristotle, he is quickly with clapping of hands driven out of the place. For of him we have learned, that the felicity of man is imperfect, except he have both the good gifts of body and of fortune. Of him we have learned, that no commonweal may flourish, in which all things are common. And we endeavour ourselves to glue fast together the decrees of this man and the doctrine of Christ--which is as likely a thing as to mingle fire and water together. And a gobbet we have received of the civil laws, because of the equity that seemeth to be in them. And to the end they should the better serve our purpose, we have, as near as may be, writhed and plied the doctrine of the gospel to them. Now by the civil law it is lawful for a man to defend violence with violence, and each to pursue for his right. Those laws approve buying and selling; they allow usury, so it be measurable; they praise war as a noble thing, so, it be just. Finally all the doctrine of Christ is so defiled with the learning of logicians, sophisters, astronomers, orators, poets, philosophers, lawyers, and gentles, that a man shall spend the most part of his life, ere he may have any leisure to search holy scripture, to the which when a man at last cometh, he must come infected with so many worldly opinions, that either he must be offended with Christ's doctrines, or else he must apply them to the mind and of them that he hath learned before. And this thing is so much approved, that it is now a heinous deed, if a man presume to study holy scripture, which hath not buried himself up to the hard ears in those trifles, or rather sophistries of Aristotle. As though Christ's doctrine were such, that it were not lawful for all men to know it, or else that it could by any means agree with the wisdom of philosophers. Besides this we admitted at the beginning of our faith some honour, which afterward we claimed as of duty. Then we received riches, but that was to distribute to relieve poor men, which afterwards we turned to our own use. And why not, since we have learned by the law civil, that the very order of charity is, that every man must first provide for himself? Nor lack there colours to cloak this

Against War and In Praise of Folly

mischief: first it is a good deed to provide for our children, and it is right that we foresee how to live in age; finally, why should we, say they, give our goods away, if we come by them without fraud? By these degrees it is by little and little come to pass, that he is taken for the best man that hath most riches: nor never was there more honour given to riches among the heathen people, than is at this day among the Christian people. For what thing is there, either spiritual or temporal, that is not done with great show of riches? And it seemed a thing agreeable with those ornaments, if Christian men had some great jurisdiction under them. Nor there wanted not such as gladly submitted themselves. Albeit at the beginning it was against their wills, and scantly would they receive it. And yet with much work, they received it so, that they were content with the name and title only: the profit thereof they gladly gave unto other men. At the last, little by little it came to pass, that a bishop thought himself no bishop, except he had some temporal lordship withal; an abbot thought himself of small authority, if he had not wherewith to play the lordly sire. And in conclusion, we blushed never a deal at the matter, we wiped away all shamefastness, and shoved aside all the bars of comeliness. And whatever abuse was used among the heathen people, were it covetousness, ambition, riot, pomp, or pride, or tyranny, the same we follow, in the same we match them, yea, and far pass them. And to pass over the lighter things for the while, I pray you, was there ever war among the heathen people so long continually, or more cruelly, than among Christian people? What stormy rumblings, what violent brays of war, what tearing of leagues, and what piteous slaughters of men have we seen ourselves within these few years? What nation hath not fought and skirmished with another? And then we go and curse the Turk; and what can be a more pleasant sight to the Turks, than to behold us daily each slaying other?

Xerxes doted, when he led out of his own country that huge multitude of people to make war upon the Greeks. Trow ye, was he not mad, when he wrote letters to the mountain called Athos, threatening that the hill should repent except it obeyed his lust? And the same Xerxes commanded also the sea to be beaten, because it was somewhat rough when he should have sailed over.

Who will deny but Alexander the Great was mad also? He, the young god, wished that there were many worlds, the which he might conquer--so great a fever of vainglory had embraced his young lusty courage. And yet these same men, the which Seneca doubted not to call mad thieves, warred after a gentler fashion than we do; they were more faithful of their promise in war, nor they used not so mischievous engines in war, nor such crafts and subtleties, nor they warred not for so light causes as we Christian men do. They rejoiced to advance and enrich such provinces as they had conquered by war; and the rude people, that lived like wild beasts without laws, learning, or good manners, they taught them both civil conditions and crafts, whereby they might live like men. In countries that were not inhabited with people, they builded cities, and made them both fair and profitable. And the places that were not very sure, they fenced, for safeguard of the people, with bridges, banks, bulwarks; and with a thousand other such commodities they helped the life of man. So that then it was right expedient to be overcome. Yea, and how many things read we, that were either wisely done, or soberly spoken of them in the midst of their wars. As for those things that are done in Christian men's wars they are more filthy and cruel than is convenient here to rehearse. Moreover, look what was worst in the heathen peoples' wars, in that we follow them, yea, we pass them.

But now it is worth while to hear, by what means we maintain this our so great madness. Thus they reason: If it had not been lawful by no means to make war, surely God would never have been the author to the Jews to make war against their enemies. Well said, but we must add hereunto, that the Jews never made war among themselves, but against strangers and wicked men. We, Christian men, fight with Christian men. Diversity of religion caused the Jews to fight against their enemies: for their enemies worshipped not God as they did. We make war oftentimes for a little childish anger, or for hunger of money, or for thirst of glory, or else for filthy meed. The Jews fought by the commandment of God; we make war to avenge the grief and displeasure of our mind. And nevertheless if men will so much lean to the example of the Jews, why do we not then in like manner use circumcision? Why do we not sacrifice with the blood of sheep and other beasts? Why do we not abstain from swine's flesh? Why doth not each of us wed many wives? Since we abhor those things, why doth the example of war please us so much? Why do we here follow the bare letter that killeth? It was permitted the Jews to make war, but so likewise as they were suffered to depart from their wives, doubtless because of their hard and froward manners. But after Christ commanded the sword to be put up, it is unlawful for Christian men to make any other war but that which is the fairest war of all, with the most eager and fierce enemies of the Church, with affection of money, with wrath, with ambition, with dread of death. These be our Philistines, these be our Nabuchodonosors, these be our Moabites and Ammonites, with the which it behooveth us to have no truce. With these we must continually fight, until (our enemies being utterly vanquished) we may be in quiet, for except we may overcome them, there is no man that may attain to any true peace, neither with himself, nor yet with no other. For this war alone is cause of true peace. He that overcometh in this battle, will make war with no man living. Nor I regard not the interpretation that some men make of the two swords, to signify either power spiritual or temporal. When Christ suffered Peter to err purposely, yea, after he was commanded to put up his sword, no man should doubt but that war was forbidden, which before seemed to be lawful. But Peter (say they) fought. True it is, Peter fought; he was yet but a Jew, and had not the spirit of a very Christian man. He fought not for his lands, or for any such titles of lands as we do, nor yet for his own life, but for his Master's life. And finally, he fought, the which within a while after forsook his Master. Now if men will needs follow the example of Peter that fought, why might they not as well follow the example of him forsaking his Master? And though Peter through simple affection erred, yet did his Master rebuke him. For else, if Christ did allow such manner of defence, as some most foolishly do interpret, why doth both all the life and doctrine of Christ preach no other thing but sufferance? Why sent he forth his disciples again tyrants, armed with nothing else but with a walking-staff and a scrip? If that sword, which Christ commanded his disciples to sell their coats to buy, be moderate defence against persecutors, like as some men do not only wickedly but also blindly interpret, why did the martyrs never use that defence? But (say they) the law of nature commandeth, it is approved by the laws, and allowed by custom, that we ought to put off from us violence by violence, and that each of us should defend his life, and eke his money, when the money (as Hesiod saith) is as lief as the life. All this I grant, but yet grace, the law of Christ, that is of more effect than all these things, commandeth us, that we should not speak ill to them that speak shrewdly to us; that we should do well to them that do ill to us, and to them that take away part of our possessions, we should give the whole; and that we should also pray for them that imagine our death. But these things (say they) appertain to the apostles; yea, they appertain to the universal people of Christ, and to the whole body of Christ's Church, that must needs be a whole and a perfect body, although in its gifts one member is more excellent than another. To them the doctrine of Christ appertaineth not, that hope not to have reward with Christ. Let them fight for money and for lordships, that laugh to scorn the saying of Christ: Blessed be the poor men in spirit; that is to say, be they poor or rich, blessed be they that covet no riches in this world. They that put all their felicity in these riches, they fight gladly to defend their life; but they be those that understand not this life to be rather a death, nor they perceive not that everlasting life is prepared for good men. Now they lay against us divers bishops of Rome, the which have been both authors and abettors of warring. True it is, some such there have been, but they were of late, and in such time as the doctrine of Christ waxed cold. Yea, and they be very few in comparison of the holy fathers that were before them, which with their writings persuade us to flee war. Why are these few examples most in mind? Why turn we our eyes from Christ to men? And why had we rather follow the uncertain examples, than the authority that is sure and certain? For doubtless the bishops of Rome were men. And it may be right well, that they were either fools or ungracious caitiffs. And yet we find not that any of them approved that we should still continually war after this fashion as we do, which thing I could with arguments prove, if I listed to digress and tarry thereupon.

    Saint Bernard praised warriors, but he so praised them, that he condemned all the manner of our warfare. And yet why should the saying of Saint Bernard, or the disputation of Thomas the Alquine, move me rather than the doctrine of Christ, which commandeth, that we should in no wise resist evil, specially under such manner as the common people do resist.

    But it is lawful (say they) that a transgressor be punished and put to death according to the laws: then is it not lawful for a whole country or city to be revenged by war? What may be answered in this place, is longer than is convenient to reply. But this much will I say, there is a great difference. For the evil-doer, found faulty and convicted, is by authority of the laws put to death. In war there is neither part without fault. Whereas one singular man doth offend, the punishment falleth only on himself; and the example of the punishment doth good unto all others. In war the most part of the punishment and harm falls upon them that least deserve to be punished; that is, upon husbandmen, old men, honest wives, young children, and virgins. But if there may any commodity at all be gathered of this most mischievous thing, that altogether goeth to the behoof of certain most vengeable thieves, hired soldiers, and strong robbers, and perhaps to a few captains, by whose craft war was raised for that intent, and with which the matter goeth never better than when the commonweal is in most high jeopardy and peril to be lost. Whereas one is for his offence grievously punished, it is the wealthy warning of all other: but in war to the end to revenge the quarrel of one, or else peradventure of a few, we cruelly afflict and grieve many thousands of them that nothing deserved. It were better to leave the offence of a few unpunished than while we seek occasion to punish one or two, to bring into assured peril and danger, both our neighbours and innocent enemies (we call them our enemies, though they never did us hurt); and yet are we uncertain, whether it shall fall on them or not, that we would have punished. It is better to let a wound alone, that cannot be cured without grievous hurt and danger of all the whole body, than go about to heal it.

    Now if any man will cry out and say: It were against all right, that he that offendeth should not be punished; hereunto I answer, that it is much more against all right and reason, that so many thousands of innocents should be brought into extreme calamity and mischief without deserving. Albeit nowadays we see, that almost all wars spring up I cannot tell of what titles, and of leagues between princes, that while they go about to subdue to their dominion some one town, they put in jeopardy all their whole empire. And yet within a while after, they sell or give away the same town again, that they got with shedding of so much blood.

Peradventure some man will say: Wouldst not have princes fight for their right? I know right well, it is not meet for such a man as I am, to dispute overboldly of princes' matters, and though I might do it without any danger, yet is it longer than is convenient for this place. But this much will I say: If each whatsoever title be a cause convenient to go in hand with war, there is no man that in so great alterations of men's affairs, and in so great variety and changes, can want a title. What nation is there that hath not sometime been put out of their own country, and also have put other out? How oft have people gone from one country to another? How oft have whole empires been translated from one to another either by chance or by league. Let the citizens of Padua claim now again in God's name the country of Troy for theirs, because Antenor was sometime a Trojan. Let the Romans now hardily claim again Africa and Spain, because those provinces were sometime under the Romans. We call that a dominion, which is but an administration. The power and authority over men, which be free by Nature, and over brute beasts, is not all one. What power and sovereignty soever you have, you have it by the consent of the people. And if I be not deceived, he that hath authority to give, hath authority to take away again. Will ye see how small a matter it is that we make all this tumult for? The strife is not, whether this city or that should be obeisant to a good prince, and not in bondage of a tyrant; but whether Ferdinand or Sigismund hath the better title to it, whether that city ought to pay tribute to Philip or to King Louis. This is that noble right, for the which all the world is thus vexed and troubled with wars and manslaughter.

Yet go to, suppose that this right or title be as strong and of as great authority as may be; suppose also there be no difference between a private field and a whole city; and admit there be no difference between the beasts that you have bought with your money and men, which be not only free, but also true Christians: yet is it a point for a wise man to cast in his mind, whether the thing that you will war for, be of so great value, that it will recompense the exceedingly great harms and loss of your own people. If you cannot do in every point as becometh a prince, yet at the leastways do as the merchantman doeth: he setteth naught by that loss, which he well perceiveth cannot be avoided without a greater loss, and he reckoneth it a winning, that fortune hath been against him with his so little loss. Or else at the leastwise follow him, of whom there is a merry tale commonly told.

There were two kinsmen at variance about dividing of certain goods, and when they could by no means agree, they must go to law together, that in conclusion the matter might be ended by sentence of the judges. They got them attorneys, the pleas were drawn, men of law had the matter in hand, they came before the judges, the complaint was entered, the cause was pleaded, and so was the war begun between them. Anon one of them remembering himself, called aside his adversary to him and said on this wise: "First it were a great shame, that a little money should dissever us twain, whom Nature hath knit so near together. Secondly, the end of our strife is uncertain, no less than of war. It is in our hands to begin when we will, but not to make an end. All our strife is but for an hundred crowns, and we shall spend the double thereof upon notaries, upon promoters, upon advocates, upon attorneys, upon judges, and upon judges' friends, if we try the law to the uttermost. We must wait upon these men, we must flatter and speak them fair, we must give them rewards. And yet I speak not of the care and thought, nor of the great labour and travail, that we must take to run about here and there to make friends; and which of us two that winneth the victory, shall be sure of more incommodity than profit. Wherefore if we be wise, let us rather see to our own profit, and the money that shall be evil bestowed upon these bribers, let us divide it between us twain. And forgive you the half of that ye think should be your due, and I will forgive as much of mine. And so shall we keep and preserve our friendship, which else is like to perish, and we shall also eschew this great business, cost, and charge. If you be not content to forgo anything of your part, I commit the whole matter into your own hands; do with it as you will. For I had liefer my friend had this money, than those insatiable thieves. Methinks I have gained enough, if I may save my good name, keep my friend, and avoid this unquiet and chargeable business." Thus partly the telling of the truth, and partly the merry conceit of his kinsman, moved the other man to agree. So they ended the matter between themselves, to the great displeasure of the judges and servants, for they, like a sort of gaping ravens, were deluded and put beside their prey.

Let a prince therefore follow the wisdom of these two men, specially in a matter of much more danger. Nor let him not regard what thing it is that he would obtain, but what great loss of good things he shall have, in what great jeopardies he shall be, and what miseries he must endure, to come thereby. Now if a man will weigh, as it were in a pair of balances, the commodities of war on the one side and the incommodities on the other side, he shall find that unjust peace is far better than righteous war. Why had we rather have war than peace? Who but a madman will angle with a golden fish-hook? If ye see that the charges and expenses shall amount far above your gain, yea, though all things go according to your mind, is it not better that ye forgo part of your right than to buy so little commodity with so innumerable mischiefs? I had liefer that any other man had the title, than I should win it with so great effusion of Christian men's blood. He (whosoever he be) hath now been many years in possession; he is accustomed to rule, his subjects know him, he behaveth him like a prince; and one shall come forth, who, finding an old title in some histories or in some blind evidence, will turn clean upside down the quiet state and good order of that commonweal. What availeth it with so great troubling to change any title, which in short space by one chance or other must go to another man? Specially since we might see, that no things in this world continue still in one state, but at the scornful pleasure of fortune they roll to and fro, as the waves of the sea. Finally, if Christian men cannot despise and set at naught these so light things, yet whereto need they by and by to run to arms? Since there be so many bishops, men of great gravity and learning; since there be so many venerable abbots; since there be so many noble men of great age, whom long use and experience of things hath made right wise: why are not these trifling and childish quarrels of princes pacified and set in order by the wisdom and discretion of these men? But they seem to make a very honest reason of war, which pretend as they would defend the Church: as though the people were not the Church, or as though the Church of Christ was begun, augmented, and stablished with wars and slaughters, and not rather in spilling of the blood of martyrs, sufferance, and despising of this life, or as though the whole dignity of the Church rested in the riches of the priests. Nor to me truly it seemeth not so allowable, that we should so oft make war upon the Turks. Doubtless it were not well with the Christian religion, if the only safeguard thereof should depend on such succours. Nor it is not likely, that they should be good Christians, that by these means are brought thereto at the first. For that thing that is got by war, is again in another time lost by war. Will ye bring the Turks to the faith of Christ? Let us not make a show of our gay riches, nor of our great number of soldiers, nor of our great strength. Let them see in us none of these solemn titles, but the assured tokens of Christian men: a pure, innocent life; a fervent desire to do well, yea, to our very enemies; the despising of money, the neglecting of glory, a poor simple life. Let them hear the heavenly doctrine agreeable to such a manner of life. These are the best armours to subdue the Turks to Christ. Now oftentimes we, being ill, fight with the evil. Yea, and I shall say another thing (which I would to God were more boldly spoken than truly), if we set aside the title and sign of the Cross, we fight Turks against Turks. If our religion were first stablished by the might and strength of men of war, if it were confirmed by dint of sword, if it were augmented by war, then let us maintain it by the same means and ways. But if all things in our faith were brought to pass by other means, why do we, then (as we mistrusted the help of Christ), seek such succour as the heathen people use? But why should we not (say they) kill them that would kill us? So think they it a great dishonour, if other should be more mischievous than they. Why do ye not, then, rob those that have robbed you before? Why do ye not scold and chide at them that rail at you? Why do ye not hate them that hate you? Trow ye it is a good Christian man's deed to slay a Turk? For be the Turks never so wicked, yet they are men, for whose salvation Christ suffered death. And killing Turks we offer to the devil most pleasant sacrifice, and with that one deed we please our enemy, the devil, twice: first because a man is slain, and again, because a Christian man slew him. There be many, which desiring to seem good Christian men, study to hurt and grieve the Turks all that ever they may; and where they be not able to do anything, they curse and ban, and bid a mischief upon them. Now by the same one point a man may perceive, that they be far from good Christian men. Succour the Turks, and where they be wicked, make them good if ye can; if ye cannot, wish and desire of God they may have grace to turn to goodness. And he that thus doeth, I will say doeth like a Christian man. But of all these things I shall entreat more largely, when I set forth my book entitled Antipolemus, which whilom when I was at Rome I wrote to Julius, bishop of Rome, the second of that name, at the same time, when he was counselled to make war on the Venetians.

But there is one thing which is more to be lamented then reasoned: That if a man would diligently discuss the matter, he shall find that all the wars among us Christian men do spring either of foolishness, or else of malice. Some young men without experience, inflamed with the evil examples of their forefathers, that they find by reading of histories, written of some foolish authors (and besides this being moved with the exhortations of flatterers, with the instigation of lawyers, and assenting thereto of the divines, the bishops winking thereat, or peradventure enticing thereunto), have rather of foolhardiness than of malice, gone in hand with war; and with the great hurt and damage of all this world they learn, that war is a thing that should be by all means and ways fled and eschewed. Some other are moved by privy hatred, ambition causeth some, and some are stirred by fierceness of mind to make war. For truly there is almost now no other thing in our cities and commonweals than is contained in Homer's work Iliad, The wrath of indiscreet princes and people.

There be those who for no other cause stir up war but to the intent they may by that means the more easily exercise tyranny on their subjects. For in the time of peace, the authority of the council, the dignity of the rulers, the vigour and strength of the laws, do somewhat hinder, that a prince cannot do all that him listeth; but as soon as war is once begun, now all the handling of matters resteth in the pleasure of a few persons. They that the prince favoureth are lifted up aloft, and they that be in his displeasure, go down. They exact as much money as pleaseth them. What need many words? Then they think themselves, that they be the greatest princes of the world. In the meantime the captains sport and play together, till they have gnawed the poor people to the hard bones. And think ye that it will grieve them, that be of this mind, to enter lightly into war, when any cause is offered? Besides all this, it is worth while to see by what means we colour our fault. I pretend the defence of our religion, but my mind is to get the great riches that the Turk hath. Under colour to defend the Church's right, I purpose to revenge the hatred that I have in my stomach. I incline to ambition, I follow my wrath; my cruel, fierce and unbridled mind compelleth me; and yet will I find a cavillation and say, the league is not kept, or friendship is broken, or something (I wot not what myself) concerning the laws of matrimony is omitted. And it is a wonder to speak, how they never obtain the very thing that they so greatly desire. And while they foolishly labour to eschew this mischief or that, they fall into another much worse, or else deeper into the same. And surely if desire of glory causeth them thus to do, it is a thing much more magnificent and glorious to save than to destroy; much more gay and goodly to build a city than to overthrow and destroy a city.

Furthermore admit that the victory in battle is got most prosperously, yet how small a portion of the glory shall go unto the prince: the commons will claim a great part of it, by the help of whose money the deed was done; foreign soldiers, that are hired for money, will challenge much more than the commons; the captains look to have very much of that glory; and fortune has the most of all, which striking a great stroke in every matter, in war may do most of all. If it come of a noble courage or stout stomach, that you be moved to make war: see, I pray you, how far wide ye be from your purpose. For while ye will not be seen to bow to one man, as to a prince your neighbour, peradventure of your alliance, who may by fortune have done you good: how much more abjectly must ye bow yourself, what time ye seek aid and help of barbarous people; yea, and, what is more unworthy, of such men as are defiled with all mischievous deeds, if we must needs call such kind of monsters men? Meanwhile ye go about to allure unto you with fair words and promises, ravishers of virgins and of religious women, men-killers, stout robbers and rovers (for these be thy special men of war). And while you labour to be somewhat cruel and superior over your equal, you are constrained to submit yourselves to the very dregs of all men living. And while ye go about to drive your neighbour out of his land, ye must needs first bring into your own land the most pestilent puddle of unthrifts that can be. You mistrust a prince of your own alliance, and will you commit yourself wholly to an armed multitude? How much surer were it to commit yourself to concord!

If ye will make war because of lucre, take your counters and cast. And I will say, it is better to have war than peace, if ye find not, that not only less, but also uncertain winning is got with inestimable costs.

Ye say ye make war for the safeguard of the commonweal, yea, but noway sooner nor more unthriftily may the commonweal perish than by war. For before ye enter into the field, ye have already hurt more your country than ye can do good getting the victory. Ye waste the citizens' goods, ye fill the houses with lamentation, ye fill all the country with thieves, robbers, and ravishers. For these are the relics of war. And whereas before ye might have enjoyed all France, ye shut yourselves from many regions thereof. If ye love your own subjects truly, why revolve you not in mind these words: Why shall I put so many, in their lusty, flourishing youth, in all mischiefs and perils? Why shall I depart so many honest wives and their husbands, and make so many fatherless children? Why shall I claim a title I know not, and a doubtful right, with spilling of my subjects' blood? We have seen in our time, that in war made under colour of defence of the Church, the priests have been so often pillaged with contributions, that no enemy might do more. So that while we go about foolishly to escape falling in the ditch, while we cannot suffer a light injury, we afflict ourselves with most grievous despites. While we be ashamed of gentleness to bow to a prince, we be fain to please people most base. While we indiscreetly covet liberty, we entangle ourselves in most grievous bondage. While we hunt after a little lucre, we grieve ourselves and ours with inestimable harness. It had been a point of a prudent Christian man (if he be a true Christian man) by all manner of means to have fled, to have shunned, and by prayer to have withstood so fiendish a thing, and so far both from the life and doctrine of Christ. But if it can by no means be eschewed, by reason of the ungraciousness of many men, when ye have essayed every way, and that ye have for peace sake left no stone unturned, then the next way is, that ye do your diligence that so ill a thing may be gested and done by them that be evil, and that it be achieved with as little effusion of man's blood as can be.

Now if we endeavour to be the selfsame thing that we hear ourselves called,--that is, good Christian men,--we shall little esteem any worldly thing, nor yet ambitiously covet anything of this world. For if we set all our mind, that we may lightly and purely part hence; if we incline wholly to heavenly things; if we pitch all our felicity in Christ alone; if we believe all that is truly good, truly gay and glorious, truly joyful, to remain in Christ alone; if we thoroughly think that a godly man can of no man be hurt; if we ponder how vain and vanishing are the scornful things of this world; if we inwardly behold how hard a thing it is for a man to be in a manner transformed into a god, and so here, with continual and indefatigable meditation, to be purged from all infections of this world, that within a while the husk of this body being cast off, it may pass hence to the company of angels; finally, if we surely have these three things, without which none is worthy of the name of a Christian man,-- Innocency, that we may be pure from all vices; Charity, that we may do good, as near as we can, to every man; Patience, that we may suffer them that do us ill, and, if we can, with good deeds overcome

Desiderius Erasmus

wrongs to us done: I pray you, what war can there be among us for trifles? If it be but a tale that is told of Christ, why do we not openly put him out of our company? Why should we glory in his title? But if he be, as he is in very deed, the true way, the very truth, and the very life, why doth all the manner of our living differ so far asunder from the true example of him? If we acknowledge and take Christ for our author, which is very Charity, and neither taught nor gave other thing but charity and peace, then go to, let us not in titles and signs, but in our deeds and living, plainly express him. Let us have in our hearts a fervent desire of peace, that Christ may again know us for his. To this intent the princes, the prelates, and the cities and commonalties should apply their counsels. There hath been hitherto enough spilt of Christian man's blood. We have showed pleasure enough to the enemies of the Christian religion. And if the common people, as they are wont, make any disturbance, let the princes bridle and quail them, which princes ought to be the selfsame thing in the commonweal that the eye is in the body, and the reason in the soul. Again, if the princes make any trouble, it is the part of good prelates by their wisdom and gravity to pacify and assuage such commotion. Or else, at the least, we being satiate with continual wars, let the desire of peace a little move us. The bishop exhorteth us (if ever any bishop did Leo the Tenth doth, which occupieth the room of our peaceable Solomon, for all his desire, all his intent and labour, is for this intent) that they whom one common faith hath coupled together, should be joined in one common concord. He laboureth that the Church of Christ should flourish, not in riches or lordships, but in her own proper virtues. Surely this is a right goodly act, and well beseeming a man descended of such a noble lineage as the Medici: by whose civil prudence the noble city of Florence most freshly flourished in long-continued peace; whose house of Medici hath been a help unto all good letters. Leo himself, having alway a sober and a gentle wit, giving himself from his tender youth to good letters of humanity, was ever brought up, as it were, in the lap of the Muses, among men most highly learned. He so faultless led his life, that even in the city of Rome, where is most liberty of vice, was of him no evil rumour, and so governing himself came to the dignity to be bishop there, which dignity he never coveted, but was chosen thereto when he least thought thereon, by the provision of God to help to redress things in great decay by long wars. Let Julius the bishop have his glory of war, victories, and of his great triumphs, the which how evil they beseem a Christian bishop, it is not for such a one as I am to declare. I will this say, his glory, whatsoever it be, was mixed with the great destruction and grievous sorrow of many a creature. But by peace restored now to the world, Leo shall get more true glory than Julius won by so many wars that he either boldly begun, or prosperously fought and achieved.

But they that had liefer hear of proverbs, than either of peace or of war, will think that I have tarried longer about this digression than is meet for the declaration of a proverb.

FINIS

In Praise of Folly
Desiderius Erasmus
Translated by John Wilson
1688

Desiderius Erasmus

Erasmus of Rotterdam to his friend

THOMAS MORE, health:

    As I was coming awhile since out of Italy for England, that I might not waste all that time I was to sit on horseback in foolish and illiterate fables, I chose rather one while to revolve with myself something of our common studies, and other while to enjoy the remembrance of my friends, of whom I left here some no less learned than pleasant. Among these you, my More, came first in my mind, whose memory, though absent yourself, gives me such delight in my absence, as when present with you I ever found in your company; than which, let me perish if in all my life I ever met with anything more delectable. And therefore, being satisfied that something was to be done, and that that time was no wise proper for any serious matter, I resolved to make some sport with the Praise of Folly. But who the devil put that in your head? you'll say. The first thing was your surname of More, which comes so near the word Moriae (Folly) as you are far from the thing. And that you are so, all the world will clear you. In the next place, I conceived this exercise of wit would not be least approved by you; inasmuch as you are wont to be delighted with such kind of mirth, that is to say, neither unlearned, if I am not mistaken, not altogether insipid, and in the whole course of your life have played the part of a Democritus. And though such is the excellence of your judgment that it was even contrary to that of the people's, yet such is your incredible affability and sweetness of temper that you both can and delight to carry yourself to all men a man of all hours. Wherefore you will not only with good will accept this small declamation, but take upon you the defense of it, for as much as being dedicated to you, it is now no longer mine but yours. But perhaps there will not be wanting some wranglers that may cavil and charge me, partly that these toys are lighter than may become a Divine, and partly more biting than may beseem the modesty of a Christian, and consequently exclaim that I resemble the ancient comedy, or another Lucian, and snarl at everything. But I would have them whom the lightness or foolery of the argument may offend to consider that mine is not the first of this kind, but the same thing that has been often practiced even by great authors: when Homer, so many ages since, did the like with the battle of frogs and mice; Virgil, with the gnat and puddings; Ovid, with the nut; when Polycrates and his corrector Isocrates extolled tyranny; Glauco, injustice; Favorinus, deformity and the quartan ague; Synescius, baldness; Lucian, the fly and flattery; when Seneca made such sport with Claudius' canonizations; Plutarch, with his dialogue between Ulysses and Gryllus; Lucian and Apuleius, with the ass; and some other, I know not who, with the hog that made his last will and testament, of which also even St. Jerome makes mention. And therefore if they please, let them suppose I played at tables for my diversion, or if they had rather have it so, that I rode on a hobbyhorse. For what injustice is it that when we allow every course of life its recreation, that study only should have none? Especially when such toys are not without their serious matter, and foolery is so handled that the reader that is not altogether thick-skulled may reap more benefit from it than from some men's crabbish and specious arguments. As when one, with long study and great pains, patches many pieces together on the praise of rhetoric or philosophy; another makes a panegyric to a prince; another encourages him to a war against the Turks; another tells you what will become of the world after himself is dead; and another finds out some new device for the better ordering of goat's wool: for as nothing is more trifling than to treat of serious matters triflingly, so nothing carries a better grace than so to discourse of trifles as a man may seem to have intended them least. For my own part, let other men judge of what I have written; though yet, unless an overweening opinion of myself may have made me blind in my own cause, I have praised folly, but not altogether foolishly. And now to say somewhat to that other cavil, of biting. This liberty was ever permitted to all men's wits, to make their smart, witty reflections on the common errors of mankind, and that too without offense, as long as this liberty does not run into licentiousness; which makes me the more admire the tender ears of the men of this age, that can away with solemn titles. No, you'll meet with some so preposterously religious that they will Sooner endure the broadest scoffs even against Christ himself than hear the Pope or a prince be touched in the least, especially if it be anything that concerns their profit; whereas he that so taxes the lives of men, without naming anyone in particular, whither, I pray, may he be said to bite, or rather to teach and admonish? Or otherwise, I beseech you, under how many notions do I tax myself? Besides, he that spares no sort of men cannot be said to be angry with anyone in particular, but the vices of all. And therefore, if there shall happen to be anyone that shall say he is hit, he will but discover either his guilt or fear. Saint Jerome sported in this kind with more freedom and greater sharpness, not sparing sometimes men's very name. But I, besides that I have wholly avoided it, I have so moderated my style that the understanding reader will easily perceive my endeavors herein were rather to make mirth than bite. Nor have I, after the example of Juvenal, raked up that forgotten sink of filth and ribaldry, but laid before you things rather ridiculous than dishonest. And now, if there be anyone that is yet dissatisfied, let him at least remember that it is no dishonor to be discommended by Folly; and having brought her in speaking, it was but fit that I kept up the character of the person. But why do I run over these things to you, a person so excellent an advocate that no man better defends his client, though the cause many times be none of the best? Farewell, my best disputant More, and stoutly defend your Moriae.

From the country,
the 5th of the Ides of June.

Desiderius Erasmus

THE PRAISE OF FOLLY

An oration, of feigned matter, spoken by Folly in her own person

At what rate soever the world talks of me (for I am not ignorant what an ill report Folly has got, even among the most foolish), yet that I am that she, that only she, whose deity recreates both gods and men, even this is a sufficient argument, that I no sooner stepped up to speak to this full assembly than all your faces put on a kind of new and unwonted pleasantness. So suddenly have you cleared your brows, and with so frolic and hearty a laughter given me your applause, that in truth as many of you as I behold on every side of me seem to me no less than Homer's gods drunk with nectar and nepenthe; whereas before, you sat as lumpish and pensive as if you had come from consulting an oracle. And as it usually happens when the sun begins to show his beams, or when after a sharp winter the spring breathes afresh on the earth, all things immediately get a new face, new color, and recover as it were a certain kind of youth again: in like manner by but beholding me you have in an instant gotten another kind of countenance; and so what the otherwise great rhetoricians with their tedious and long-studied orations can hardly effect, to wit, to remove the trouble of the mind, I have done it at once with my single look.

But if you ask me why I appear before you in this strange dress, be pleased to lend me your ears, and I'll tell you; not those ears, I mean, you carry to church, but abroad with you, such as you are wont to prick up to jugglers, fools, and buffoons, and such as our friend Midas once gave to Pan. For I am disposed awhile to play the Sophist with you; not of their sort who nowadays boozle young men's heads with certain empty notions and curious trifles, yet teach them nothing but a more than womanish obstinacy of scolding: but I'll imitate those ancients who, that they might the better avoid that infamous appellation of Sophi or Wise chose rather to be called Sophists. Their business was to celebrate the praises of the gods and valiant men. And the like encomium shall you hear from me, but neither of Hercules nor Solon, but my own dear self, that is to say, Folly. Nor do I esteem those wisemen a rush that call it a foolish and insolent thing to praise one's self. Be it as foolish as they would make it, so they confess it proper: and what can be more than that Folly be her own trumpet? For who can set me out better than myself, unless perhaps I could be better known to another than to myself? Though yet I think it somewhat more modest than the general practice of our nobles and wise men who, throwing away all shame, hire some flattering orator or lying poet from whose mouth they may hear their praises, that is to say, mere lies; and yet, composing themselves with a seeming modesty, spread out their peacock's plumes and erect their crests, while this impudent flatterer equals a man of nothing to the gods and proposes him as an absolute pattern of all virtue that's wholly a stranger to it, sets out a pitiful jay in other's feathers, washes the Blackmoor white, and lastly swells a gnat to an elephant. In short, I will follow that old proverb that says, "He may lawfully praise himself that lives far from neighbors." Though, by the way, I cannot but wonder at the ingratitude, shall I say, or negligence of men who, notwithstanding they honor me in the first place and are willing enough to confess my bounty, yet not one of them for these so many ages has there been who in some thankful oration has set out the praises of Folly; when yet there has not wanted them whose elaborate endeavors have extolled tyrants, agues, flies, baldness, and such other pests of nature, to their own loss of both time and sleep. And now you shall hear from me a plain extemporary speech, but so much the truer. Nor would I have you think it like the rest of orators, made for the ostentation of wit; for these, as you know, when they have been beating their heads some thirty years about an oration and at last perhaps produce somewhat that was never their own, shall yet swear they composed it in three days, and that too for diversion: whereas I ever liked it best to speak whatever came first out.

But let none of you expect from me that after the manner of rhetoricians I should go about to define what I am, much less use any division; for I hold it equally unlucky to circumscribe her whose deity is universal, or make the least division in that worship about which everything is so generally agreed. Or to what purpose, think you, should I describe myself when I am here present before you, and you behold me speaking? For I am, as you see, that true and only giver of wealth whom the Greeks call Moria, the Latins Stultitia, and our plain English Folly. Or what need was there to have said so much, as if my very looks were not sufficient to inform you who I am? Or as if any man, mistaking me for Wisdom, could not at first sight convince himself by my face, the true index of my mind? I am no counterfeit, nor do I carry one thing in my looks and an other in my breast. No, I am in every respect so like myself that neither can they dissemble me who arrogate to themselves the appearance and title of wise men and walk like asses in scarlet hoods, though after all their hypocrisy Midas' ears will discover their master. A most ungrateful generation of men that, when they are wholly given up to my party, are yet publicly ashamed of the name, as taking it for a reproach; for which cause, since in truth they are morotatoi, fools, and yet would appear to the world to be wise men and Thales, we'll even call them morosophous, wise fools.

    Nor will it be amiss also to imitate the rhetoricians of our times, who think themselves in a manner gods if like horse leeches they can but appear to be double-tongued, and believe they have done a mighty act if in their Latin orations they can but shuffle in some ends of Greek like mosaic work, though altogether by head and shoulders and less to the purpose. And if they want hard words, they run over some worm-eaten manuscript and pick out half a dozen of the most old and obsolete to confound their reader, believing, no doubt, that they that understand their meaning will like it the better, and they that do not, will admire it more by how much less they understand it. Nor is this way of ours of admiring what seems foreign without its particular grace; for if there happen to be any more ambitious than others, they may give their applause with a smile, and, like the ass, shake their ears, that they may be thought to understand more than the rest of their neighbors.

    But to come to the purpose: I have given you my name, but what epithet shall I add? What but that of the most foolish? For by what more proper name can so great a goddess as Folly be known to her disciples? And because it is not alike known to all from what stock I am sprung, with the Muses' good leave I'll do my endeavor to satisfy you. But yet neither the first Chaos, Orcus, Saturn, or Japhet, nor any of those threadbare, musty gods were my father, but Plutus, Riches; that only he, that is, in spite of Hesiod, Homer, nay and Jupiter himself, divum pater atque hominum rex, the father of gods and men, at whose single beck, as heretofore, so at present, all things sacred and profane are turned topsy-turvy. According to whose pleasure war, peace, empire, counsels, judgments, assemblies, wedlocks, bargains, leagues, laws, arts, all things light or serious--I want breath--in short, all the public and private business of mankind is governed; without whose help all that herd of gods of the poets' making, and those few of the better sort of the rest, either would not be at all, or if they were, they would be but such as live at home and keep a poor house to themselves. And to whomsoever he's an enemy, 'tis not Pallas herself that can befriend him; as on the contrary he whom he favors may lead Jupiter and his thunder in a string. This is my father and in him I glory. Nor did he produce me from his brain, as Jupiter that sour and ill-looked Pallas; but of that lovely nymph called Youth, the most beautiful and galliard of all the rest. Not was I, like that limping blacksmith, begot in the sad and irksome bonds of matrimony. Yet, mistake me not, 'twas not that blind and decrepit Plutus in Aristophanes that got me, but such as he was in his full strength and pride of youth; and not that only, but at such a time when he had been well heated with nectar, of which he had, at one of the banquets of the gods, taken a dose extraordinary.

    And as to the place of my birth, forasmuch as nowadays that is looked upon as a main point of nobility, it was neither, like Apollo's, in the floating Delos, nor Venus-like on the rolling sea, nor in any of blind Homer's as blind caves: but in the Fortunate Islands, where all things grew without plowing or sowing; where neither labor, nor old age, nor disease was ever heard of; and in whose fields neither daffodil, mallows, onions, beans, and such contemptible things would ever grow, but, on the contrary, rue, angelica, bugloss, marjoram, trefoils, roses, violets, lilies, and all the gardens of Adonis invite both your sight and your smelling. And being thus born, I did not begin the world, as other children are wont, with crying; but straight perched up and smiled on my mother. Nor do I envy to the great Jupiter the goat, his nurse, forasmuch as I was suckled by two jolly nymphs, to wit, Drunkenness, the daughter of Bacchus, and Ignorance, of Pan. And as for such my companions and followers as you perceive about me, if you have a mind to know who they are, you are not like to be the wiser for me, unless it be in Greek: this here, which you observe with that proud cast of her eye, is Philautia, Self-love; she with the smiling countenance, that is ever and anon clapping her hands, is Kolakia, Flattery; she that looks as if she were half asleep is Lethe, Oblivion; she that sits leaning on both elbows with her hands clutched together is Misoponia, Laziness; she with the garland on her head, and that smells so strong of perfumes, is Hedone, Pleasure; she with those staring eyes, moving here and there, is Anoia, Madness; she with the smooth skin and full pampered body is Tryphe, Wantonness; and, as to the two gods that you see with them, the one is Komos, Intemperance, the other Ecgretos hypnos, Dead Sleep. These, I say, are my household servants, and by their faithful counsels I have subjected all things to my dominion and erected an empire over emperors themselves. Thus have you had my lineage, education, and companions.

    And now, lest I may seem to have taken upon me the name of goddess without cause, you shall in the next place understand how far my deity extends, and what advantage by it I have brought both to gods and men. For, if it was not unwisely said by somebody, that this only is to be a god, to help men; and if they are deservedly enrolled among the gods that first brought in corn and wine and such other things as are for the common good of mankind, why am not I of right the alpha, or first, of all the gods? who being but one, yet bestow all things on all men. For first, what is more sweet or more precious than life? And yet from whom can it more properly be said to come than from me? For neither the crab-

Desiderius Erasmus

favoured Pallas' spear nor the cloudgathering Jupiter's shield either beget or propagate mankind; but even he himself, the father of gods and king of men at whose very beck the heavens shake, must lay by his forked thunder and those looks wherewith he conquered the giants and with which at pleasure he frightens the rest of the gods, and like a common stage player put on a disguise as often as he goes about that, which now and then he does, that is to say the getting of children: And the Stoics too, that conceive themselves next to the gods, yet show me one of them, nay the veriest bigot of the sect, and if he do not put off his beard, the badge of wisdom, though yet it be no more than what is common with him and goats; yet at least he must lay by his supercilious gravity, smooth his forehead, shake off his rigid principles, and for some time commit an act of folly and dotage. In fine, that wise man whoever he be, if he intends to have children, must have recourse to me. But tell me, I beseech you, what man is that would submit his neck to the noose of wedlock, if, as wise men should, he did but first truly weigh the inconvenience of the thing? Or what woman is there would ever go to it did she seriously consider either the peril of child-bearing or the trouble of bringing them up? So then, if you owe your beings to Wedlock, you owe that wedlock to this my follower, Madness; and what you owe to me I have already told you. Again, she that has but once tried what it is, would she, do you think, make a second venture if it were not for my other companion, Oblivion? Nay, even Venus herself, notwithstanding whatever Lucretius has said, would not deny but that all her virtue were lame and fruitless without the help of my deity. For out of that little, odd, ridiculous May-game came the supercilious philosophers, in whose room have succeeded a kind of people the world calls monks, cardinals, priests, and the most holy popes. And lastly, all that rabble of the poets' gods, with which heaven is so thwacked and thronged, that though it be of so vast an extent, they are hardly able to crowd one by another.

But I think it is a small matter that you thus owe your beginning of life to me, unless I also show you that whatever benefit you receive in the progress of it is of my gift likewise. For what other is this? Can that be called life where you take away pleasure? Oh! Do you like what I say? I knew none of you could have so little wit, or so much folly, or wisdom rather, as to be of any other opinion. For even the Stoics themselves that so severely cried down pleasure did but handsomely dissemble, and railed against it to the common people to no other end but that having discouraged them from it, they might the more plentifully enjoy it themselves. But tell me, by Jupiter, what part of man's life is that that is not sad, crabbed, unpleasant, insipid, troublesome, unless it be seasoned with pleasure, that is to say, folly? For the proof of which the never sufficiently praised Sophocles in that his happy elegy of us, "To know nothing is the only happiness," might be authority enough, but that I intend to take every particular by itself.

And first, who knows not but a man's infancy is the merriest part of life to himself, and most acceptable to others? For what is that in them which we kiss, embrace, cherish, nay enemies succor, but this witchcraft of folly, which wise Nature did of purpose give them into the world with them that they might the more pleasantly pass over the toil of education, and as it were flatter the care and diligence of their nurses? And then for youth, which is in such reputation everywhere, how do all men favor it, study to advance it, and lend it their helping hand? And whence, I pray, all this grace? Whence but from me? by whose kindness, as it understands as little as may be, it is also for that reason the higher privileged from exceptions; and I am mistaken if, when it is grown up and by experience and discipline brought to savor something like man, if in the same instant that beauty does not fade, its liveliness decay, its pleasantness grow fat, and its briskness fail. And by how much the further it runs from me, by so much the less it lives, till it comes to the burden of old age, not only hateful to others, but to itself also. Which also were altogether insupportable did not I pity its condition, in being present with it, and, as the poets' gods were wont to assist such as were dying with some pleasant metamorphosis, help their decrepitness as much as in me lies by bringing them back to a second childhood, from whence they are not improperly called Twice-children. Which, if you ask me how I do it, I shall not be shy in the point. I bring them to our River Lethe (for its springhead rises in the Fortunate Islands, and that other of hell is but a brook in comparison), from which, as soon as they have drunk down a long forgetfulness, they wash away by degrees the perplexity of their minds, and so wax young again.

But perhaps you'll say they are foolish and doting. Admit it; 'tis the very essence of childhood; as if to be such were not to be a fool, or that that condition had anything pleasant in it, but that it understood nothing. For who would not look upon that child as a prodigy that should have as much wisdom as a man?--according to that common proverb, "I do not like a child that is a man too soon." Or who would endure a converse or friendship with that old man who to so large an experience of things had joined an equal strength of mind and sharpness of judgment? And therefore for this reason it is that old age dotes; and that it does so, it is beholding to me. Yet, not withstanding, is this dotard exempt from all those cares that distract a wise man; he is not the less pot-companion, nor is he sensible of that burden of life which the more manly age finds enough to do to stand upright under it. And sometimes too, like Plautus' Old-man, he returns to his three letters, A.M.O., the most unhappy of all things living, if he rightly understood what he did in it. And yet, so much do I befriend him that I make him well received of his friends and no unpleasant companion; for as much as, according to Homer, Nestor's discourse was pleasanter than honey, whereas Achilles' was both bitter and malicious; and that of Old-men, as he has it in another place, florid. In which respect also they have this advantage of children, in that they want the only pleasure of the others' life, we'll suppose it prattling. Add to this that old men are more eagerly delighted with children, and they, again, with Old-men. "Like to like," quoted the Devil to the collier. For what difference between them, but that the one has more wrinkles and years upon his head than the other? Otherwise, the brightness of their hair, toothless mouth, weakness of body, love of milk, broken speech, chatting, toying, forgetfulness, inadvertency, and briefly, all other their actions agree in everything. And by how much the nearer they approach to this old age, by so much they grow backward into the likeness of children, until like them they pass from life to death, without any weariness of the one, or sense of the other.

And now, let him that will compare the benefits they receive by me, the metamorphoses of the gods, of whom I shall not mention what they have done in their pettish humors but where they have been most favorable: turning one into a tree, another into a bird, a third into a grasshopper, serpent, or the like. As if there were any difference between perishing and being another thing! But I restore the same man to the best and happiest part of his life. And if men would but refrain from all commerce with wisdom and give up themselves to be governed by me, they should never know what it were to be old, but solace themselves with a perpetual youth. Do but observe our grim philosophers that are perpetually beating their brains on knotty subjects, and for the most part you'll find them grown old before they are scarcely young. And whence is it, but that their continual and restless thoughts insensibly prey upon their spirits and dry up their radical moisture? Whereas, on the contrary, my fat fools are as plump and round as a Westphalian hog, and never sensible of old age, unless perhaps, as sometimes it rarely happens, they come to be infected with wisdom, so hard a thing it is for a man to be happy in all things. And to this purpose is that no small testimony of the proverb, that says, "Folly is the only thing that keeps youth at a stay and old age afar off;" as it is verified in the Brabanders, of whom there goes this common saying, "That age, which is wont to render other men wiser, makes them the greater fools." And yet there is scarce any nation of a more jocund converse, or that is less sensible of the misery of old age, than they are. And to these, as in situation, so for manner of living, come nearest my friends the Hollanders. And why should I not call them mine, since they are so diligent observers of me that they are commonly called by my name?--of which they are so far from being ashamed, they rather pride themselves in it. Let the foolish world then be packing and seek out Medeas, Circes, Venuses, Auroras, and I know not what other fountains of restoring youth. I am sure I am the only person that both can, and have, made it good. 'Tis I alone that have that wonderful juice with which Memnon's daughter prolonged the youth of her grandfather Tithon. I am that Venus by whose favor Phaon became so young again that Sappho fell in love with him. Mine are those herbs, if yet there be any such, mine those charms, and mine that fountain that not only restores departed youth but, which is more desirable, preserves it perpetual. And if you all subscribe to this opinion, that nothing is better than youth or more execrable than age, I conceive you cannot but see how much you are indebted to me, that have retained so great a good and shut out so great an evil.

But why do I altogether spend my breath in speaking of mortals? View heaven round, and let him that will, reproach me with my name, if he find any one of the gods that were not stinking and contemptible, were he not made acceptable by my deity. Why is it that Bacchus is always a stripling, and bushy-haired? but because he is mad, and drunk, and spends his life in drinking, dancing, revels, and May games, not having so much as the least society with Pallas. And lastly, he is so far from desiring to be accounted wise that he delights to be worshipped with sports and gambols; nor is he displeased with the proverb that gave him the surname of fool, "A greater fool than Bacchus;" which name of his was changed to Morychus, for that sitting before the gates of his temple, the wanton country people were wont to bedaub him with new wine and figs. And of scoffs, what not, have not the ancient comedies thrown on him? O foolish god, say they, and worthy to be born as you were of your father's thigh! And yet, who had not rather be your fool and sot, always merry, ever young, and making sport for other people, than either Homer's Jupiter with his crooked counsels, terrible to everyone; or old Pan with his hubbubs; or smutty Vulcan half covered with cinders; or even Pallas herself, so dreadful with her Gorgon's head and spear and a countenance like bullbeef? Why is Cupid always portrayed like a boy, but because he is a very wag and can neither do nor so much as think of anything sober? Why Venus ever in her prime, but because of her affinity with me? Witness that color of her hair, so resembling my father, from whence she is called the golden Venus; and lastly, ever laughing, if you give any credit to the poets, or their followers the statuaries. What deity did the Romans ever more religiously adore than that of Flora, the foundress of all pleasure? Nay, if you should but diligently search the lives of the most sour and morose of the gods out of Homer and the test of the poets, you would find them all but so many pieces of Folly. And to what purpose should I run over any of the other gods' tricks when you know enough of Jupiter's loose loves? When that chaste Diana shall so far forget her sex as to be ever hunting and ready to perish for Endymion? But I had rather they should hear these things from Momus, from whom heretofore they were wont to have their shares, till in one of their angry humors they tumbled him, together with Ate, goddess of mischief, down headlong to the earth, because his wisdom, forsooth, unseasonably disturbed their happiness. Nor since that dares any mortal give him harbor, though I must confess there wanted little but that he had been received into the courts of princes, had not my companion Flattery reigned in chief there, with whom and the other there is no more correspondence than between lambs and wolves. From whence it is that the gods play the fool with the greater liberty and more content to themselves "doing all things carelessly," as says Father Homer, that is to say, without anyone to correct them. For what ridiculous stuff is there which that stump of the fig tree Priapus does not afford them? What tricks and legerdemains with which Mercury does not cloak his thefts? What buffoonery that Vulcan is not guilty of, while one with his polt-foot, another with his smutched muzzle, another with his impertinencies, he makes sport for the rest of the gods? As also that old Silenus with his country dances, Polyphemus footing time to his Cyclops hammers, the nymphs with their jigs and satyrs with their antics; while Pan makes them all twitter with some coarse ballad, which yet they had rather hear than the Muses themselves, and chiefly when they are well whittled with nectar. Besides, what should I mention what these gods do when they are half drunk? Now by my troth, so foolish that I myself can hardly refrain laughter. But in these matters 'twere better we remembered Harpocrates, lest some eavesdropping god or other take us whispering that which Momus only has the privilege of speaking at length.

And therefore, according to Homer's example, I think it high time to leave the gods to themselves, and look down a little on the earth; wherein likewise you'll find nothing frolic or fortunate that it owes not to me. So provident has that great parent of mankind, Nature, been that there should not be anything without its mixture and, as it were, seasoning of Folly. For since according to the definition of the Stoics, wisdom is nothing else than to be governed by reason, and on the contrary Folly, to be given up to the will of our passions, that the life of man might not be altogether disconsolate and hard to away with, of how much more passion than reason has Jupiter composed us? putting in, as one would say, "scarce half an ounce to a pound." Besides, he has confined reason to a narrow corner of the brain and left all the rest of the body to our passions; has also set up, against this one, two as it were, masterless tyrants--anger, that possesses the region of the heart, and consequently the very fountain of life, the heart itself; and lust, that stretches its empire everywhere. Against which double force how powerful reason is let common experience declare, inasmuch as she, which yet is all she can do, may call out to us till she be hoarse again and tell us the rules of honesty and virtue; while they give up the reins to their governor and make a hideous clamor, till at last being wearied, he suffer himself to be carried whither they please to hurry him.

But forasmuch as such as are born to the business of the world have some little sprinklings of reason more than the rest, yet that they may the better manage it, even in this as well as in other things, they call me to counsel; and I give them such as is worthy of myself, to wit, that they take to them a wife--a silly thing, God wot, and foolish, yet wanton and pleasant, by which means the roughness of the masculine temper is seasoned and sweetened by her folly. For in that Plato seems to doubt under what genus he should put woman, to wit, that of rational creatures or brutes, he intended no other in it than to show the apparent folly of the sex. For if perhaps any of them goes about to be thought wiser than the rest, what else does she do but play the fool twice, as if a man should "teach a cow to dance," "a thing quite against the hair." For as it doubles the crime if anyone should put a disguise upon Nature, or endeavor to bring her to that she will in no wise bear, according to that proverb of the Greeks, "An ape is an ape, though clad in scarlet;" so a woman is a woman still, that is to say foolish, let her put on whatever vizard she please.

But, by the way, I hope that sex is not so foolish as to take offense at this, that I myself, being a woman, and Folly too, have attributed folly to them. For if they weigh it right, they needs must acknowledge that they owe it to folly that they are more fortunate than men. As first their beauty, which, and that not without cause, they prefer before everything, since by its means they exercise a tyranny even upon tyrants themselves; otherwise, whence proceeds that sour look, rough skin, bushy beard, and such other things as speak plain old age in a man, but from that disease of wisdom? Whereas women's cheeks are ever plump and smooth, their voice small, their skin soft, as if they imitated a certain kind of perpetual youth. Again, what greater thing do they wish in their whole lives than that they may please the men? For to what other purpose are all those dresses, washes, baths, curlings, slops, perfumes, and those several little tricks of setting their faces, painting their eyebrows, and smoothing their skins? And now tell me, what higher letters of recommendation have they to men than this folly? For what is it they do not permit them to do? And to what other purpose than that of pleasure? Wherein yet their folly is not the least thing that pleases; which so true it is, I think no one will deny, that does but consider with himself, what foolish discourse and odd gambols pass between a man and his woman, as often as he had a mind to be gamesome? And so I have shown you whence the first and chiefest delight of man's life springs.

But there are some, you'll say, and those too none of the youngest, that have a greater kindness for the pot than the petticoat and place their chiefest pleasure in good fellowship. If there can be any great entertainment without a woman at it, let others look to it. This I am sure, there was never any pleasant which folly gave not the relish to. Insomuch that if they find no occasion of laughter, they send for "one that may make it," or hire some buffoon flatterer, whose ridiculous discourse may put by the gravity of the company. For to what purpose were it to clog our stomachs with dainties, junkets, and the like stuff, unless our eyes and ears, nay whole mind, were likewise entertained with jests, merriments, and laughter? But of these kind of second courses I am the only cook; though yet those ordinary practices of our feasts, as choosing a king, throwing dice, drinking healths, trolling it round, dancing the cushion, and the like, were not invented by the seven wise men but myself, and that too for the common pleasure of mankind. The nature of all which things is such that the more of folly they have, the more they conduce to human life, which, if it were unpleasant, did not deserve the name of life; and other than such it could not well be, did not these kind of diversions wipe away tediousness, next cousin to the other.

But perhaps there are some that neglect this way of pleasure and rest satisfied in the enjoyment of their friends, calling friendship the most desirable of all things, more necessary than either air, fire, or water; so delectable that he that shall take it out of the world had as good put out the sun; and, lastly, so commendable, if yet that make anything to the matter, that neither the philosophers themselves doubted to reckon it among their chiefest good. But what if I show you that I am both the beginning and end of this so great good also? Nor shall I go about to prove it by fallacies, sorites, dilemmas, or other the like subtleties of logicians, but after my blunt way point out the thing as clearly as it were with my finger.

And now tell me if to wink, slip over, be blind at, or deceived in the vices of our friends, nay, to admire and esteem them for virtues, be not at least the next degree to folly? What is it when one kisses his mistress' freckle neck, another the wart on her nose? When a father shall swear his squint-eyed child is more lovely than Venus? What is this, I say, but mere folly? And so, perhaps you'll cry it is; and yet 'tis this only that joins friends together and continues them so joined. I speak of ordinary men, of whom none are born without their imperfections, and happy is he that is pressed with the least: for among wise princes there is either no friendship at all, or if there be, 'tis unpleasant and reserved, and that too but among a very few 'twere a crime to say none. For that the greatest part of mankind are fools, nay there is not anyone that dotes not in many things; and friendship, you know, is seldom made but among equals. And yet if it should so happen that there were a mutual good will between them, it is in no wise firm nor very long lived; that is to say, among such as are morose and more circumspect than needs, as being eagle-sighted into his friends' faults, but so blear-eyed to their own that they take not the least notice of the wallet that hangs behind their own shoulders. Since then the nature of man is such that there is scarce anyone to be found that is not subject to many errors, add to this the great diversity of minds and studies, so many slips, oversights, and chances of human life, and how is it possible there should be any true friendship between those Argus, so much as one hour, were it not for that which the Greeks excellently call euetheian? And you may render by folly or good nature, choose you whether. But what? Is not the author and parent of all our love, Cupid, as blind as a beetle? And as with him all colors agree, so from him is it that everyone likes his own sweeterkin best, though never so ugly, and "that an old man dotes on his old wife, and a boy on his girl." These things are not only done everywhere but laughed at too; yet as ridiculous as they are, they make society pleasant, and, as it were, glue it together.

And what has been said of friendship may more reasonably be presumed of matrimony, which in truth is no other than an inseparable conjunction of life. Good God! What divorces, or what not worse than that, would daily happen were not the converse between a man and his wife supported and cherished by flattery, apishness, gentleness, ignorance, dissembling, certain retainers of mine also! Whoop holiday! how few marriages should we have, if the husband should but thoroughly examine how many tricks his pretty little mop of modesty has played before she was married! And how fewer of them would hold together, did not most of the wife's actions escape the husband's knowledge through his neglect or sottishness! And for this also you are beholden to me, by whose means it is that the husband is pleasant to his wife, the wife to her husband, and the house kept in quiet. A man is laughed at, when seeing his wife weeping he licks up her tears. But how much happier is it to be thus deceived than by being troubled with jealousy not only to torment himself but set all things in a hubbub!

In fine, I am so necessary to the making of all society and manner of life both delightful and lasting, that neither would the people long endure their governors, nor the servant his master, nor the master his footman, nor the scholar his tutor, nor one friend another, nor the wife her husband, nor the usurer the borrower, nor a soldier his commander, nor one companion another, unless all of them had their interchangeable failings, one while flattering, other while prudently conniving, and generally sweetening one another with some small relish of folly.

And now you'd think I had said all, but you shall hear yet greater things. Will he, I pray, love anyone that hates himself? Or ever agree with another who is not at peace with himself? Or beget pleasure in another that is troublesome to himself? I think no one will say it that is not more foolish than Folly. And yet, if you should exclude me, there's no man but would be so far from enduring another that he would stink in his own nostrils, be nauseated with his own actions, and himself become odious to himself; forasmuch as Nature, in too many things rather a stepdame than a parent to us, has imprinted that evil in men, especially such as have least judgment, that everyone repents him of his own condition and admires that of others. Whence it comes to pass that all her gifts, elegancy, and graces corrupt and perish. For what benefit is beauty, the greatest blessing of heaven, if it be mixed with affectation? What youth, if corrupted with the severity of old age?

Lastly, what is that in the whole business of a man's life he can do with any grace to himself or others --for it is not so much a thing of art, as the very life of every action, that it be done with a good meen--unless this my friend and companion, Self-love, be present with it? Nor does she without cause supply me the place of a sister, since her whole endeavors are to act my part everywhere. For what is more foolish than for a man to study nothing else than how to please himself? To make himself the object of his own admiration? And yet, what is there that is either delightful or taking, nay rather what not the contrary, that a man does against the hair? Take away this salt of life, and the orator may even sit still with his action, the musician with all his division will be able to please no man, the player be hissed off the stage, the poet and all his Muses ridiculous, the painter with his art contemptible, and the physician with all his slip-slops go a-begging. Lastly, you will be taken for an ugly fellow instead of a beautiful, for old and decrepit instead of youthful, and a beast instead of a wise man, a child instead of eloquent, and instead of a well-bred man, a clown. So necessary a thing it is that everyone flatter himself and commend himself to himself before he can be commended by others.

Lastly, since it is the chief point of happiness "that a man is willing to be what he is," you have further abridged in this my Self-love, that no man is ashamed of his own face, no man of his own wit, no man of his own parentage, no man of his own house, no man of his manner of living, not any man of his own country; so that a Highlander has no desire to change with an Italian, a Thracian with an Athenian, not a Scythian for the Fortunate Islands. O the singular care of Nature, that in so great a variety of things has made all equal! Where she has been sometimes sparing of her gifts she has recompensed it with the mote of self-love; though here, I must confess, I speak foolishly, it being the greatest of all other her gifts: to say nothing that no great action was ever attempted without my motion, or art brought to perfection without my help.

Is not war the very root and matter of all famed enterprises? And yet what more foolish than to undertake it for I know what trifles, especially when both parties are sure to lose more than they get by the bargain? For of those that are slain, not a word of them; and for the rest, when both sides are close engaged "and the trumpets make an ugly noise," what use of those wise men, I pray, that are so exhausted with study that their thin, cold blood has scarce any spirits left? No, it must be those blunt, fat fellows, that by how much the more they exceed in courage, fall short in understanding. Unless perhaps one had rather choose Demosthenes for a soldier, who, following the example of Archilochius, threw away his arms and betook him to his heels e'er he had scarce seen his enemy; as ill a soldier, as happy an orator.

But counsel, you'll say, is not of least concern in matters of war. In a general I grant it; but this thing of warring is not part of philosophy, but managed by parasites, panders, thieves, cut-throats, plowmen, sots, spendthrifts, and such other dregs of mankind, not philosophers; who how unapt they are even for common converse, let Socrates, whom the oracle of Apollo, though not so wisely, judged "the wisest of all men living," be witness; who stepping up to speak somewhat, I know not what, in public was forced to come down again well laughed at for his pains. Though yet in this he was not altogether a fool, that he refused the appellation of wise, and returning it back to the oracle, delivered his opinion that a wise man should abstain from meddling with public business; unless perhaps he should have rather admonished us to beware of wisdom if we intended to be reckoned among the number of men, there being nothing but his wisdom that first accused and afterwards sentenced him to the drinking of his poisoned cup. For while, as you find him in Aristophanes, philosophizing about clouds and ideas, measuring how far a flea could leap, and admitting that so small a creature as a fly should make so great a buzz, he meddled not with anything that concerned common life. But his master being in danger of his head, his scholar Plato is at hand, to wit that famous patron, that being disturbed with the noise of the people, could not go through half his first sentence. What should I speak of Theophrastus, who being about to make an oration, became as dumb as if he had met a wolf in his way, which yet would have put courage in a man of war? Or Isocrates, that was so cowhearted that he dared never attempt it? Or Tully, that great founder of the Roman eloquence, that could never begin to speak without an odd kind of trembling, like a boy that had got the hiccough; which Fabius interprets as an argument of a wise orator and one that was sensible of what he was doing; and while he says it, does he not plainly confess that wisdom is a great obstacle to the true management of business? What would become of them, think you, were they to fight it out at blows that are so dead through fear when the contest is only with empty words?

And next to these is cried up, forsooth, that goodly sentence of Plato's, "Happy is that commonwealth where a philosopher is prince, or whose prince is addicted to philosophy." When yet if you consult historians, you'll find no princes more pestilent to the commonwealth than where the empire has fallen to some smatterer in philosophy or one given to letters. To the truth of which I think the Catoes give sufficient credit; of whom the one was ever disturbing the peace of the commonwealth with his hair-brained accusations; the other, while he too wisely vindicated its liberty, quite overthrew it. Add to this the Bruti, Cassii, nay Cicero himself, that was no less pernicious to the commonwealth of Rome than was Demosthenes to that of Athens. Besides M. Antoninus (that I may give you one instance that there was once one good emperor; for with much ado I can make it out) was become burdensome and hated of his subjects upon no other score but that he was so great a philosopher. But admitting him good, he did the commonwealth more hurt in leaving behind him such a son as he did than ever he did it good by his own government. For these kind of men that are so given up to the study of wisdom are generally most unfortunate, but chiefly in their children; Nature, it seems, so providently ordering it, lest this mischief of wisdom should spread further among mankind. For which reason it is manifest why Cicero's son was so degenerate, and that wise Socrates' children, as one has well observed, were more like their mother than their father, that is to say, fools.

However this were to be born with, if only as to public employments they were "like a sow upon a pair of organs," were they anything more apt to discharge even the common offices of life. Invite a wise man to a feast and he'll spoil the company, either with morose silence or troublesome disputes. Take him out to dance, and you'll swear "a cow would have done it better." Bring him to the theatre, and his very looks are enough to spoil all, till like Cato he take an occasion of withdrawing rather than put off his supercilious gravity. Let him fall into discourse, and he shall make more sudden stops than if he had a wolf before him. Let him buy, or sell, or in short go about any of those things without which there is no living in this world, and you'll say this piece of wisdom were rather a stock than a man, of so little use is he to himself, country, or friends; and all because he is wholly ignorant of common things and lives a course of life quite different from the people; by which means it is impossible but that he contract a popular odium, to wit, by reason of the great diversity of their life and souls. For what is there at all done among men that is not full of folly, and that too from fools and to fools? Against which universal practice if any single one shall dare to set up his throat, my advice to him is, that following the example of Timon, he retire into some desert and there enjoy his wisdom to himself.

But, to return to my design, what power was it that drew those stony, oaken, and wild people into cities but flattery? For nothing else is signified by Amphion and Orpheus' harp. What was it that, when the common people of Rome were like to have destroyed all by their mutiny, reduced them to obedience? Was it a philosophical oration? Least. But a ridiculous and childish fable of the belly and the rest of the members. And as good success had Themistocles in his of the fox and hedgehog. What wise man's oration could ever have done so much with the people as Sertorius' invention of his white hind? Or his ridiculous emblem of pulling off a horse's tail hair by hair? Or as Lycurgus his example of his two whelps? To say nothing of Minos and Numa, both which ruled their foolish multitudes with fabulous inventions; with which kind of toys that great and powerful beast, the people, are led anyway. Again what city ever received Plato's or Aristotle's laws, or Socrates' precepts? But, on the contrary, what made the Decii devote themselves to the infernal gods, or Q. Curtius to leap into the gulf, but an empty vainglory, a most bewitching siren? And yet 'tis strange it should be so condemned by those wise philosophers. For what is more foolish, say they, than for a suppliant suitor to flatter the people, to buy their favor with gifts, to court the applauses of so many fools, to please himself with their acclamations, to be carried on the people's shoulders as in triumph, and have a brazen statue in the marketplace? Add to this the adoption of names and surnames, those divine honors given to a man of no reputation, and the deification of the most wicked tyrants with public ceremonies; most foolish things, and such as one Democritus is too little to laugh at. Who denies it? And yet from this root sprang all the great acts of the heroes which the pens of so many eloquent men have extolled to the skies. In a word, this folly is that that laid the foundation of cities; and by it, empire, authority, religion, policy, and public actions are preserved; neither is there anything in human life that is not a kind of pastime of folly.

But to speak of arts, what set men's wits on work to invent and transmit to posterity so many famous, as they conceive, pieces of learning but the thirst of glory? With so much loss of sleep, such pains and travail, have the most foolish of men thought to purchase themselves a kind of I know not what fame, than which nothing can be more vain. And yet notwithstanding, you owe this advantage to folly, and which is the most delectable of all other, that you reap the benefit of other men's madness.

And now, having vindicated to myself the praise of fortitude and industry, what think you if I do the same by that of prudence? But some will say, you may as well join fire and water. It may be so. But yet I doubt not but to succeed even in this also, if, as you have done hitherto, you will but favor me with your attention. And first, if prudence depends upon experience, to whom is the honor of that name more proper? To the wise man, who partly out of modesty and partly distrust of himself, attempts nothing; or the fool, whom neither modesty which he never had, nor danger which he never considers, can discourage from anything? The wise man has recourse to the books of the ancients, and from thence picks nothing but subtleties of words. The fool, in undertaking and venturing on the business of the world, gathers, if I mistake not, the true prudence, such as Homer though blind may be said to have seen when he said, "The burnt child dreads the fire." For there are two main obstacles to the knowledge of things, modesty that casts a mist before the understanding, and fear that, having fancied a danger, dissuades us from the attempt. But from these folly sufficiently frees us, and few there are that rightly understand of what great advantage it is to blush at nothing and attempt everything.

But if you had rather take prudence for that that consists in the judgment of things, hear me, I beseech you, how far they are from it that yet crack of the name. For first 'tis evident that all human things, like Alcibiades' Sileni or rural gods, carry a double face, but not the least alike; so that what at first sight seems to be death, if you view it narrowly may prove to be life; and so the contrary. What appears beautiful may chance to be deformed; what wealthy, a very beggar; what infamous, praiseworthy; what learned, a dunce; what lusty, feeble; what jocund, sad; what noble, base; what lucky, unfortunate; what friendly, an enemy; and what healthful, noisome. In short, view the inside of these Sileni, and you'll find them quite other than what they appear; which, if perhaps it shall not seem so philosophically spoken, I'll make it plain to you "after my blunt way." Who would not conceive a prince a great lord and abundant in everything? But yet being so ill-furnished with the gifts of the mind, and ever thinking he shall never have enough, he's the poorest of all men. And then for his mind so given up to vice, 'tis a shame how it enslaves him. I might in like manner philosophize of the rest; but let this one, for example's sake, be enough.

Yet why this? will someone say. Have patience, and I'll show you what I drive at. If anyone seeing a player acting his part on a stage should go about to strip him of his disguise and show him to the people in his true native form, would he not, think you, not only spoil the whole design of the play, but deserve himself to be pelted off with stones as a phantastical fool and one out of his wits? But nothing is more common with them than such changes; the same person one while impersonating a woman, and another while a man; now a youngster, and by and by a grim seignior; now a king, and presently a peasant; now a god, and in a trice again an ordinary fellow. But to discover this were to spoil all, it being the only thing that entertains the eyes of the spectators. And what is all this life but a kind of comedy, wherein men walk up and down in one another's disguises and act their respective parts, till the property-man brings them back to the attiring house. And yet he often orders a different dress, and makes him that came but just now off in the robes of a king put on the rags of a beggar. Thus are all things represented by counterfeit, and yet without this there was no living.

And here if any wise man, as it were dropped from heaven, should start up and cry, this great thing whom the world looks upon for as a god and I know not what is not so much as a man, for that like a beast he is led by his passions, but the worst of slaves, inasmuch as he gives himself up willingly to so many and such detestable masters. Again if he should bid a man that were bewailing the death of his father to laugh, for that he now began to live by having got an estate, without which life is but a kind of death; or call another that were boasting his family ill begotten or base, because he is so far removed from virtue that is the only fountain of nobility; and so of the rest: what else would he get by it but be thought himself mad and frantic? For as nothing is more foolish than preposterous wisdom, so nothing is more unadvised than a forward unseasonable prudence. And such is his that does not comply with the present time "and order himself as the market goes," but forgetting that law of feasts, "either drink or begone," undertakes to disprove a common received opinion. Whereas on the contrary 'tis the part of a truly prudent man not to be wise beyond his condition, but either to take no notice of what the world does, or run with it for company. But this is foolish, you'll say; nor shall I deny it, provided always you be so civil on the other side as to confess that this is to act a part in that world.

But, O you gods, "shall I speak or hold my tongue?" But why should I be silent in a thing that is more true than truth itself? However it might not be amiss perhaps in so great an affair to call forth the Muses from Helicon, since the poets so often invoke them upon every foolish occasion. Be present then awhile, and assist me, you daughters of Jupiter, while I make it out that there is no way to that so much famed wisdom, nor access to that fortress as they call it of happiness, but under the banner of Folly. And first 'tis agreed of all hands that our passions belong to Folly; inasmuch as we judge a wise man from a fool by this, that the one is ordered by them, the other by reason; and therefore the Stoics remove from a wise man all disturbances of mind as so many diseases. But these passions do not only the office of a tutor to such as are making towards the port of wisdom, but are in every exercise of virtue as it were spurs and incentives, nay and encouragers to well doing: which though that great Stoic Seneca most strongly denies, and takes from a wise man all affections whatever, yet in doing that he leaves him not so much as a man but rather a new kind of god that was never yet nor ever like to be. Nay, to speak plainer, he sets up a stony semblance of a man, void of all sense and common feeling of humanity. And much good to them with this wise man of theirs; let them enjoy him to themselves, love him without competitors, and live with him in Plato's commonwealth, the country of ideas, of Tantalus' orchards. For who would not shun and startle at such a man, as at some unnatural accident or spirit? A man dead to all sense of nature and common affections, and no more moved with love or pity than if he were a flint or rock; whose censure nothing escapes; that commits no errors himself, but has a lynx's eyes upon others; measures everything by an exact line, and forgives nothing; pleases himself with himself only; the only rich, the only wise, the only free man, and only king; in brief, the only man that is everything, but in his own single judgment only; that cares not for the friendship of any man, being himself a friend to no man; makes no doubt to make the gods stoop to him, and condemns and laughs at the whole actions of our life? And yet such a beast is this their perfect wise man. But tell me pray, if the thing were to be carried by most voices, what city would choose him for its governor, or what army desire him for their general? What woman would have such a husband, what goodfellow such a guest, or what servant would either wish or endure such a master? Nay, who had not rather have one of the middle sort of fools, who, being a fool himself, may the better know how to command or obey fools; and who though he please his like, 'tis yet the greater number; one that is kind to his wife, merry among his friends, a boon companion, and easy to be lived with; and lastly one that thinks nothing of humanity should be a stranger to him? But I am weary of this wise man, and therefore I'll proceed to some other advantages.

    Go to then. Suppose a man in some lofty high tower, and that he could look round him, as the poets say Jupiter was now and then wont. To how many misfortunes would he find the life of man subject? How miserable, to say no worse, our birth, how difficult our education; to how many wrongs our childhood exposed, to what pains our youth; how unsupportable our old age, and grievous our unavoidable death? As also what troops of diseases beset us, how many casualties hang over our heads, how many troubles invade us, and how little there is that is not steeped in gall? To say nothing of those evils one man brings upon another, as poverty, imprisonment, infamy, dishonesty, racks, snares, treachery, reproaches, actions, deceits--but I'm got into as endless a work as numbering the sands--for what offenses mankind have deserved these things, or what angry god compelled them to be born into such miseries is not my present business. Yet he that shall diligently examine it with himself, would he not, think you, approve the example of the Milesian virgins and kill himself? But who are they that for no other reason but that they were weary of life have hastened their own fate? Were they not the next neighbors to wisdom? among whom, to say nothing of Diogenes, Xenocrates, Cato, Cassius, Brutus, that wise man Chiron, being offered immortality, chose rather to die than be troubled with the same thing always.

    And now I think you see what would become of the world if all men should be wise; to wit it were necessary we got another kind of clay and some better potter. But I, partly through ignorance, partly unadvisedness, and sometimes through forgetfulness of evil, do now and then so sprinkle pleasure with the hopes of good and sweeten men up in their greatest misfortunes that they are not willing to leave this life,. even then when according to the account of the destinies this life has left them; and by how much the less reason they have to live, by so much the more they desire it; so far are they from being sensible of the least wearisomeness of life. Of my gift it is, that you have so many old Nestors everywhere that have scarce left them so much as the shape of a man; stutterers, dotards, toothless, grayhaired, bald; or rather, to use the words of Aristophanes, "Nasty, crumpled, miserable, shriveled, bald, toothless, and wanting their baubles," yet so delighted with life and to be thought young that one dyes his gray hairs; another covers his baldness with a periwig; another gets a set of new teeth; another falls desperately in love with a young wench and keeps more flickering about her than a young man would have been ashamed of. For to see such an old crooked piece with one foot in the grave to marry a plump young wench, and that too without a portion, is so common that men almost expect to be commended for it. But the best sport of all is to see our old women, even dead with age, and such skeletons one would think they had stolen out of their graves, and ever mumbling in their mouths, "Life is sweet;" and as old as they are, still caterwauling, daily plastering their face, scarce ever from the glass, gossiping, dancing, and writing love letters. These things are laughed at as foolish, as indeed they are; yet they please themselves, live merrily, swim in pleasure, and in a word are happy, by my courtesy. But I would have them to whom these things seem ridiculous to consider with themselves whether it be not better to live so pleasant a life in such kind of follies, than, as the proverb goes, "to take a halter and hang themselves." Besides though these things may be subject to censure, it concerns not my fools in the least, inasmuch as they take no notice of it; or if they do, they easily neglect it. If a stone fall upon a man's head, that's evil indeed; but dishonesty, infamy, villainy, ill reports carry no more hurt in them than a man is sensible of; and if a man have no sense of them, they are no longer evils. What are you the worse if the people hiss at you, so you applaud yourself? And that a man be able to do so, he must owe it to folly.

    But methinks I hear the philosophers opposing it and saying 'tis a miserable thing for a man to be foolish, to err, mistake, and know nothing truly. Nay rather, this is to be a man. And why they should call it miserable, I see no reason; forasmuch as we are so born, so bred, so instructed, nay such is the common condition of us all. And nothing can be called miserable that suits with its kind, unless perhaps you'll think a man such because he can neither fly with birds, nor walk on all four with beasts, and is not armed with horns as a bull. For by the same reason he would call the warlike horse unfortunate, because he understood not grammar, nor ate cheese-cakes; and the bull miserable, because he'd make so ill a wrestler. And therefore, as a horse that has no skill in grammar is not miserable, no more is man in this respect, for that they agree with his nature. But again, the virtuosi may say that there was particularly added to man the knowledge of sciences, by whose help he might recompense himself in understanding for what nature cut him short in other things. As if this had the least face of truth, that Nature that was so solicitously watchful in the production of gnats, herbs, and flowers should have so slept when she made man, that he should have need to be helped by sciences, which that old devil Theuth, the evil genius of mankind, first invented for his destruction, and are so little conducive to happiness that they rather obstruct it; to which purpose they are properly said to be first found out, as that wise king in Plato argues touching the invention of letters.

Sciences therefore crept into the world with other the pests of mankind, from the same head from whence all other mischiefs spring; we'll suppose it devils, for so the name imports when you call them demons, that is to say, knowing. For that simple people of the golden age, being wholly ignorant of everything called learning, lived only by the guidance and dictates of nature; for what use of grammar, where every man spoke the same language and had no further design than to understand one another? What use of logic, where there was no bickering about the double-meaning words? What need of rhetoric, where there were no lawsuits? Or to what purpose laws, where there were no ill manners? from which without doubt good laws first came. Besides, they were more religious than with an impious curiosity to dive into the secrets of nature, the dimension of stars, the motions, effects, and hidden causes of things; as believing it a crime for any man to attempt to be wise beyond his condition. And as to the inquiry of what was beyond heaven, that madness never came into their heads. But the purity of the golden age declining by degrees, first, as I said before, arts were invented by the evil genii; and yet but few, and those too received by fewer. After that the Chaldean superstition and Greek newfangledness, that had little to do, added I know not how many more; mere torments of wit, and that so great that even grammar alone is work enough for any man for his whole life.

Though yet among these sciences those only are in esteem that come nearest to common sense, that is to say, folly. Divines are half starved, naturalists out of heart, astrologers laughed at, and logicians slighted; only the physician is worth all the rest. And among them too, the more unlearned, impudent, or unadvised he is, the more he is esteemed, even among princes. For physic, especially as it is now professed by most men, is nothing but a branch of flattery, no less than rhetoric. Next them, the second place is given to our law-drivers, if not the first, whose profession, though I say it myself, most men laugh at as the ass of philosophy; yet there's scarce any business, either so great or so small, but is managed by these asses. These purchase their great lordships, while in the meantime the divine, having run through the whole body of divinity, sits gnawing a radish and is in continual warfare with lice and fleas. As therefore those arts are best that have the nearest affinity with folly, so are they most happy of all others that have least commerce with sciences and follow the guidance of Nature, who is in no wise imperfect, unless perhaps we endeavor to leap over those bounds she has appointed to us. Nature hates all false coloring and is ever best where she is least adulterated with art.

Go to then, don't you find among the several kinds of living creatures that they thrive best that understand no more than what Nature taught them? What is more prosperous or wonderful than the bee? And though they have not the same judgment of sense as other bodies have, yet wherein has architecture gone beyond their building of houses? What philosopher ever founded the like republic? Whereas the horse, that comes so near man in understanding and is therefore so familiar with him, is also partaker of his misery. For while he thinks it a shame to lose the race, it often happens that he cracks his wind; and in the battle, while he contends for victory, he's cut down himself, and, together with his rider "lies biting the earth;" not to mention those strong bits, sharp spurs, close stables, arms, blows, rider, and briefly, all that slavery he willingly submits to, while, imitating those men of valor, he so eagerly strives to be revenged of the enemy. Than which how much more were the life of flies or birds to be wished for, who living by the instinct of nature, look no further than the present, if yet man would but let them alone in it. And if at anytime they chance to be taken, and being shut up in cages endeavor to imitate our speaking, 'tis strange how they degenerate from their native gaiety. So much better in every respect are the works of nature than the adulteries of art.

In like manner I can never sufficiently praise that Pythagoras in a dunghill cock, who being but one had been yet everything, a philosopher, a man, a woman, a king, a private man, a fish, a horse, a frog, and, I believe too, a sponge; and at last concluded that no creature was more miserable than man, for that all other creatures are content with those bounds that nature set them, only man endeavors to exceed them. And again, among men he gives the precedency not to the learned or the great, but the fool. Nor had that Gryllus less wit than Ulysses with his many counsels, who chose rather to lie grunting in a hog sty than be exposed with the other to so many hazards. Nor does Homer, that father of trifles, dissent from me; who not only called all men "wretched and full of calamity," but often his great pattern of wisdom, Ulysses, "miserable;" Paris, Ajax, and Achilles nowhere. And why, I pray but that, like a cunning fellow and one that was his craft's master, he did nothing without the advice of Pallas? In a word he was too wise, and by that means ran wide of nature. As therefore among men they are least happy that study wisdom, as being in this twice fools, that when they are born men, they should yet so far forget their condition as to affect the life of gods; and after the example of the giants, with their

Against War and In Praise of Folly

philosophical gimcracks make a war upon nature: so they on the other side seem as little miserable as is possible who come nearest to beasts and never attempt anything beyond man. Go to then, let's try how demonstrable this is; not by enthymemes or the imperfect syllogisms of the Stoics, but by plain, downright, and ordinary examples.

And now, by the immortal gods! I think nothing more happy than that generation of men we commonly call fools, idiots, lack-wits, and dolts; splendid titles too, as I conceive them. I'll tell you a thing, which at first perhaps may seem foolish and absurd, yet nothing more true. And first they are not afraid of death--no small evil, by Jupiter! They are not tormented with the conscience of evil acts, not terrified with the fables of ghosts, nor frightened with spirits and goblins. They are not distracted with the fear of evils to come nor the hopes of future good. In short, they are not disturbed with those thousand of cares to which this life is subject. They are neither modest, nor fearful, nor ambitious, nor envious, nor love they any man. And lastly, if they should come nearer even to the very ignorance of brutes, they could not sin, for so hold the divines. And now tell me, you wise fool, with how many troublesome cares your mind is continually perplexed; heap together all the discommodities of your life, and then you'll be sensible from how many evils I have delivered my fools. Add to this that they are not only merry, play, sing, and laugh themselves, but make mirth wherever they come, a special privilege it seems the gods have given them to refresh the pensiveness of life. Whence it is that whereas the world is so differently affected one towards another, that all men indifferently admit them as their companions, desire, feed, cherish, embrace them, take their parts upon all occasions, and permit them without offense to do or say what they like. And so little does everything desire to hurt them, that even the very beasts, by a kind of natural instinct of their innocence no doubt, pass by their injuries. For of them it may be truly said that they are consecrate to the gods, and therefore and not without cause do men have them in such esteem. Whence is it else that they are in so great request with princes that they can neither eat nor drink, go anywhere, or be an hour without them? Nay, and in some degree they prefer these fools before their crabbish wise men, whom yet they keep about them for state's sake. Nor do I conceive the reason so difficult, or that it should seem strange why they are preferred before the others, for that these wise men speak to princes about nothing but grave, serious matters, and trusting to their own parts and learning do not fear sometimes "to grate their tender ears with smart truths;" but fools fit them with that they most delight in, as jests, laughter, abuses of other men, wanton pastimes, and the like.

Again, take notice of this no contemptible blessing which Nature has given fools, that they are the only plain, honest men and such as speak truth. And what is more commendable than truth? For though that proverb of Alcibiades in Plato attributes truth to drunkards and children, yet the praise of it is particularly mine, even from the testimony of Euripides, among whose other things there is extant that his honorable saying concerning us, "A fool speaks foolish things." For whatever a fool has in his heart, he both shows it in his looks and expresses it in his discourse; while the wise men's are those two tongues which the same Euripides mentions, whereof the one speaks truth, the other what they judge most seasonable for the occasion. These are they "that turn black into white," blow hot and cold with the same breath, and carry a far different meaning in their breast from what they feign with their tongue. Yet in the midst of all their prosperity, princes in this respect seem to me most unfortunate, because, having no one to tell them truth, they are forced to receive flatterers for friends.

But, someone may say, the ears of princes are strangers to truth, and for this reason they avoid those wise men, because they fear lest someone more frank than the rest should dare to speak to them things rather true than pleasant; for so the matter is, that they don't much care for truth. And yet this is found by experience among my fools, that not only truths but even open reproaches are heard with pleasure; so that the same thing which, if it came from a wise man's mouth might prove a capital crime, spoken by a fool is received with delight. For truth carries with it a certain peculiar power of pleasing, if no accident fall in to give occasion of offense; which faculty the gods have given only to fools. And for the same reasons is it that women are so earnestly delighted with this kind of men, as being more propense by nature to pleasure and toys. And whatsoever they may happen to do with them, although sometimes it be of the most serious, yet they turn it to jest and laughter, as that sex was ever quickwitted, especially to color their own faults.

But to return to the happiness of fools, who when they have passed over this life with a great deal of pleasantness and without so much as the least fear or sense of death, they go straight forth into the Elysian field, to recreate their pious and careless souls with such sports as they used here. Let's proceed then, and compare the condition of any of your wise men with that of this fool. Fancy to me now some example of wisdom you'd set up against him; one that had spent his childhood and youth in learning the sciences and lost the sweetest part of his life in watchings, cares, studies, and for the remaining part of it never so much as tasted the least of pleasure; ever sparing, poor, sad, sour, unjust, and rigorous to himself, and troublesome and hateful to others; broken with paleness, leanness, crassness, sore eyes, and an old age and death contracted before their time (though yet, what matter is it, when he die that never lived?); and such is the picture of this great wise man.

And here again do those frogs of the Stoics croak at me and say that nothing is more miserable

Desiderius Erasmus

than madness. But folly is the next degree, if not the very thing. For what else is madness than for a man to be out of his wits? But to let them see how they are clean out of the way, with the Muses' good favor we'll take this syllogism in pieces. Subtly argued, I must confess, but as Socrates in Plato teaches us how by splitting one Venus and one Cupid to make two of either, in like manner should those logicians have done and distinguished madness from madness, if at least they would be thought to be well in their wits themselves. For all madness is not miserable, or Horace had never called his poetical fury a beloved madness; nor Plato placed the raptures of poets, prophets, and lovers among the chiefest blessings of this life; nor that sibyl in Virgil called Aeneas' travels mad labors. But there are two sorts of madness, the one that which the revengeful Furies send privily from hell, as often as they let loose their snakes and put into men's breasts either the desire of war, or an insatiate thirst after gold, or some dishonest love, or parricide, or incest, or sacrilege, or the like plagues, or when they terrify some guilty soul with the conscience of his crimes; the other, but nothing like this, that which comes from me and is of all other things the most desirable; which happens as often as some pleasing dotage not only clears the mind of its troublesome cares but renders it more jocund. And this was that which, as a special blessing of the gods, Cicero, writing to his friend Atticus, wished to himself, that he might be the less sensible of those miseries that then hung over the commonwealth.

Nor was that Grecian in Horace much wide of it, who was so far mad that he would sit by himself whole days in the theatre laughing and clapping his hands, as if he had seen some tragedy acting, whereas in truth there was nothing presented; yet in other things a man well enough, pleasant among his friends, kind to his wife, and so good a master to his servants that if they had broken the seal of his bottle, he would not have run mad for it. But at last, when by the care of his friends and physic he was freed from his distemper and become his own man again, he thus expostulates with them, "Now, by Pollux, my friends, you have rather killed than preserved me in thus forcing me from my pleasure." By which you see he liked it so well that he lost it against his will. And trust me, I think they were the madder of the two, and had the greater need of hellebore, that should offer to look upon so pleasant a madness as an evil to be removed by physic; though yet I have not determined whether every distemper of the sense or understanding be to be called madness.

For neither he that having weak eyes should take a mule for an ass, nor he that should admire an insipid poem as excellent would be presently thought mad; but he that not only errs in his senses but is deceived also in his judgment, and that too more than ordinary and upon all occasions--he, I must confess, would be thought to come very near to it. As if anyone hearing an ass bray should take it for excellent music, or a beggar conceive himself a king. And yet this kind of madness, if, as it commonly happens, it turn to pleasure, it brings a great delight not only to them that are possessed with it but to those also that behold it, though perhaps they may not be altogether so mad as the other, for the species of this madness is much larger than the people take it to be. For one mad man laughs at another, and beget themselves a mutual pleasure. Nor does it seldom happen that he that is the more mad, laughs at him that is less mad. And in this every man is the more happy in how many respects the more he is mad; and if I were judge in the case, he should be ranged in that class of folly that is peculiarly mine, which in truth is so large and universal that I scarce know anyone in all mankind that is wise at all hours, or has not some tang or other of madness.

And to this class do they appertain that slight everything in comparison of hunting and protest they take an unimaginable pleasure to hear the yell of the horns and the yelps of the hounds, and I believe could pick somewhat extraordinary out of their very excrement. And then what pleasure they take to see a buck or the like unlaced? Let ordinary fellows cut up an ox or a wether, 'twere a crime to have this done by anything less than a gentleman! who with his hat off, on his bare knees, and a couteau for that purpose (for every sword or knife is not allowable), with a curious superstition and certain postures, lays open the several parts in their respective order; while they that hem him in admire it with silence, as some new religious ceremony, though perhaps they have seen it a hundred times before. And if any of them chance to get the least piece of it, he presently thinks himself no small gentleman. In all which they drive at nothing more than to become beasts themselves, while yet they imagine they live the life of princes.

And next these may be reckoned those that have such an itch of building; one while changing rounds into squares, and presently again squares into rounds, never knowing either measure or end, till at last, reduced to the utmost poverty, there remains not to them so much as a place where they may lay their head, or wherewith to fill their bellies. And why all this? but that they may pass over a few years in feeding their foolish fancies.

And, in my opinion, next these may be reckoned such as with their new inventions and occult arts undertake to change the forms of things and hunt all about after a certain fifth essence; men so bewitched with this present hope that it never repents them of their pains or expense, but are ever contriving how they may cheat themselves, till, having spent all, there is not enough left them to provide another furnace. And yet they have not done dreaming these their pleasant dreams but encourage others, as much as in them lies, to the same happiness. And at last, when they are quite lost in all their expectations, they cheer up themselves with this sentence, "In great things the very attempt is enough," and then complain of the shortness of man's life that is not sufficient for so great an understanding.

And then for gamesters, I am a little doubtful whether they are to be admitted into our college; and yet 'tis a foolish and ridiculous sight to see some addicted so to it that they can no sooner hear the rattling of the dice but their heart leaps and dances again. And then when time after time they are so far drawn on with the hopes of winning that they have made shipwreck of all, and having split their ship on that rock of dice, no less terrible than the bishop and his clerks, scarce got alive to shore, they choose rather to cheat any man of their just debts than not pay the money they lost, lest otherwise, forsooth, they be thought no men of their words. Again what is it, I pray, to see old fellows and half blind to play with spectacles? Nay, and when a justly deserved gout has knotted their knuckles, to hire a caster, or one that may put the dice in the box for them? A pleasant thing, I must confess, did it not for the most part end in quarrels, and therefore belongs rather to the Furies than me.

But there is no doubt but that that kind of men are wholly ours who love to hear or tell feigned miracles and strange lies and are never weary of any tale, though never so long, so it be of ghosts, spirits, goblins, devils, or the like; which the further they are from truth, the more readily they are believed and the more do they tickle their itching ears. And these serve not only to pass away time but bring profit, especially to mass priests and pardoners. And next to these are they that have gotten a foolish but pleasant persuasion that if they can but see a wooden or painted Polypheme Christopher, they shall not die that day; or do but salute a carved Barbara, in the usual set form, that he shall return safe from battle; or make his application to Erasmus on certain days with some small wax candles and proper prayers, that he shall quickly be rich. Nay, they have gotten a Hercules, another Hippolytus, and a St. George, whose horse most religiously set out with trappings and bosses there wants little but they worship; however, they endeavor to make him their friend by some present or other, and to swear by his master's brazen helmet is an oath for a prince. Or what should I say of them that hug themselves with their counterfeit pardons; that have measured purgatory by an hourglass, and can without the least mistake demonstrate its ages, years, months, days, hours, minutes, and seconds, as it were in a mathematical table? Or what of those who, having confidence in certain magical charms and short prayers invented by some pious impostor, either for his soul's health or profit's sake, promise to themselves everything: wealth, honor, pleasure, plenty, good health, long life, lively old age, and the next place to Christ in the other world, which yet they desire may not happen too soon, that is to say before the pleasures of this life have left them?

And now suppose some merchant, soldier, or judge, out of so many rapines, parts with some small piece of money. He straight conceives all that sink of his whole life quite cleansed; so many perjuries, so many lusts, so many debaucheries, so many contentions, so many murders, so many deceits, so many breaches of trusts, so many treacheries bought off, as it were by compact; and so bought off that they may begin upon a new score. But what is more foolish than those, or rather more happy, who daily reciting those seven verses of the Psalms promise to themselves more than the top of felicity? Which magical verses some devil or other, a merry one without doubt but more a blab of his tongue than crafty, is believed to have discovered to St. Bernard, but not without a trick. And these are so foolish that I am half ashamed of them myself, and yet they are approved, and that not only by the common people but even the professors of religion. And what, are not they also almost the same where several countries avouch to themselves their peculiar saint, and as everyone of them has his particular gift, so also his particular form of worship? As, one is good for the toothache; another for groaning women; a third, for stolen goods; a fourth, for making a voyage prosperous; and a fifth, to cure sheep of the rot; and so of the rest, for it would be too tedious to run over all. And some there are that are good for more things than one; but chiefly, the Virgin Mother, to whom the common people do in a manner attribute more than to the Son.

Yet what do they beg of these saints but what belongs to folly? To examine it a little. Among all those offerings which are so frequently hung up in churches, nay up to the very roof of some of them, did you ever see the least acknowledgment from anyone that had left his folly, or grown a hair's breadth the wiser? One escapes a shipwreck, and he gets safe to shore. Another, run through in a duel, recovers. Another, while the rest were fighting, ran out of the field, no less luckily than valiantly. Another, condemned to be hanged, by the favor of some saint or other, a friend to thieves, got off himself by impeaching his fellows. Another escaped by breaking prison. Another recovered from his fever in spite of his physician. Another's poison turning to a looseness proved his remedy rather than death; and that to his wife's no small sorrow, in that she lost both her labor and her charge. Another's cart broke, and he saved his horses. Another preserved from the fall of a house. All these hang up their tablets, but no one gives thanks for his recovery from folly; so sweet a thing it is not to be wise, that on the contrary men rather pray against anything than folly.

But why do I launch out into this ocean of superstitions? Had I a hundred tongues, as many mouths, and a voice never so strong, yet were I not able to run over the several sorts of fools or all the names of folly, so thick do they swarm everywhere. And yet your priests make no scruple to receive and

Desiderius Erasmus

cherish them as proper instruments of profit; whereas if some scurvy wise fellow should step up and speak things as they are, as, to live well is the way to die well; the best way to get quit of sin is to add to the money you give the hatred of sin, tears, watchings, prayers, fastings, and amendment of life; such or such a saint will favor you, if you imitate his life-- these, I say, and the like--should this wise man chat to the people, from what happiness into how great troubles would he draw them?

Of this college also are they who in their lifetime appoint with what solemnity they'll be buried, and particularly set down how many torches, how many mourners, how many singers, how many almsmen they will have at it; as if any sense of it could come to them, or that it were a shame to them that their corpse were not honorably interred; so curious are they herein, as if, like the aediles of old, these were to present some shows or banquet to the people.

And though I am in haste, yet I cannot yet pass by them who, though they differ nothing from the meanest cobbler, yet 'tis scarcely credible how they flatter themselves with the empty title of nobility. One derives his pedigree from Aeneas, another from Brutus, a third from the star by the tail of Ursa Major. They show you on every side the statues and pictures of their ancestors; run over their great-grandfathers and the great-great-grandfathers of both lines, and the ancient matches of their families, when themselves yet are but once removed from a statue, if not worse than those trifles they boast of. And yet by means of this pleasant self-love they live a happy life. Nor are they less fools who admire these beasts as if they were gods.

But what do I speak of any one or the other particular kind of men, as if this self-love had not the same effect everywhere and rendered most men superabundantly happy? As when a fellow, more deformed than a baboon, shall believe himself handsomer than Homer's Nereus. Another, as soon as he can draw two or three lines with a compass, presently thinks himself a Euclid. A third, that understands music no more than my horse, and for his voice as hoarse as a dunghill cock, shall yet conceive himself another Hermogenes. But of all madness that's the most pleasant when a man, seeing another any way excellent in what he pretends to himself, makes his boasts of it as confidently as if it were his own. And such was that rich fellow in Seneca, who whenever he told a story had his servants at his elbow to prompt him the names; and to that height had they flattered him that he did not question but he might venture a rubber at cuffs, a man otherwise so weak he could scarce stand, only presuming on this, that he had a company of sturdy servants about him.

Or to what purpose is it I should mind you of our professors of arts? Forasmuch as this self-love is so natural to them all that they had rather part with their father's land than their foolish opinions; but chiefly players, fiddlers, orators, and poets, of which the more ignorant each of them is, the more insolently he pleases himself, that is to say vaunts and spreads out his plumes. And like lips find like lettuce; nay, the more foolish anything is, the more 'tis admired, the greater number being ever tickled at the worst things, because, as I said before, most men are so subject to folly. And therefore if the more foolish a man is, the more he pleases himself and is admired by others, to what purpose should he beat his brains about true knowledge, which first will cost him dear, and next render him the more troublesome and less confident, and lastly, please only a few?

And now I consider it, Nature has planted, not only in particular men but even in every nation, and scarce any city is there without it, a kind of common self-love. And hence is it that the English, besides other things, particularly challenge to themselves beauty, music, and feasting. The Scots are proud of their nobility, alliance to the crown, and logical subtleties. The French think themselves the only wellbred men. The Parisians, excluding all others, arrogate to themselves the only knowledge of divinity. The Italians affirm they are the only masters of good letters and eloquence, and flatter themselves on this account, that of all others they only are not barbarous. In which kind of happiness those of Rome claim the first place, still dreaming to themselves of somewhat, I know not what, of old Rome. The Venetians fancy themselves happy in the opinion of their nobility. The Greeks, as if they were the only authors of sciences, swell themselves with the titles of the ancient heroes. The Turk, and all that sink of the truly barbarous, challenge to themselves the only glory of religion and laugh at Christians as superstitious. And much more pleasantly the Jews expect to this day the coming of the Messiah, and so obstinately contend for their Law of Moses. The Spaniards give place to none in the reputation of soldiery. The Germans pride themselves in their tallness of stature and skill in magic.

And, not to instance in every particular, you see, I conceive, how much satisfaction this Self-love, who has a sister also not unlike herself called Flattery, begets everywhere; for self-love is no more than the soothing of a man's self, which, done to another, is flattery. And though perhaps at this day it may be thought infamous, yet it is so only with them that are more taken with words than things. They think truth is inconsistent with flattery, but that it is much otherwise we may learn from the examples of brute beasts. What more fawning than a dog? And yet what more trusty? What has more of those little tricks than a squirrel? And yet what more loving to man? Unless, perhaps you'll say, men had better converse with fierce lions, merciless tigers, and furious leopards. For that flattery is the most pernicious of all things, by means of which some treacherous persons and mockers have run the credulous into such mischief. But this of mine proceeds from a certain gentleness and uprightness of mind and comes nearer

Against War and In Praise of Folly

to virtue than its opposite, austerity, or a morose and troublesome peevishness, as Horace calls it. This supports the dejected, relieves the distressed, encourages the fainting, awakens the stupid, refreshes the sick, supplies the untractable, joins loves together, and keeps them so joined. It entices children to take their learning, makes old men frolic, and, under the color of praise, does without offense both tell princes their faults and show them the way to amend them. In short, it makes every man the more jocund and acceptable to himself, which is the chiefest point of felicity. Again, what is more friendly than when two horses scrub one another? And to say nothing of it, that it's a main part of physic, and the only thing in poetry; 'tis the delight and relish of all human society.

But 'tis a sad thing, they say, to be mistaken. Nay rather, he is most miserable that is not so. For they are quite beside the mark that place the happiness of men in things themselves, since it only depends upon opinion. For so great is the obscurity and variety of human affairs that nothing can be clearly known, as it is truly said by our academics, the least insolent of all the philosophers; or if it could, it would but obstruct the pleasure of life. Lastly, the mind of man is so framed that it is rather taken with the false colors than truth; of which if anyone has a mind to make the experiment, let him go to church and hear sermons, in which if there be anything serious delivered, the audience is either asleep, yawning, or weary of it; but if the preacher--pardon my mistake, I would have said declaimer--as too often it happens, fall but into an old wives' story, they're presently awake, prick up their ears and gape after it. In like manner, if there be any poetical saint, or one of whom there goes more stories than ordinary, as for example, a George, a Christopher, or a Barbara, you shall see him more religiously worshipped than Peter, Paul, or even Christ himself. But these things are not for this place.

And now at how cheap a rate is this happiness purchased! Forasmuch as to the thing itself a man's whole endeavor is required, be it never so inconsiderable; but the opinion of it is easily taken up, which yet conduces as much or more to happiness. For suppose a man were eating rotten stockfish, the very smell of which would choke another, and yet believed it a dish for the gods, what difference is there as to his happiness? Whereas on the contrary, if another's stomach should turn at a sturgeon, wherein, I pray, is he happier than the other? If a man have a crooked, ill-favored wife, who yet in his eye may stand in competition with Venus, is it not the same as if she were truly beautiful? Or if seeing an ugly, ill-pointed piece, he should admire the work as believing it some great master's hand, were he not much happier, think you, than they that buy such things at vast rates, and yet perhaps reap less pleasure from them than the other? I know one of my name that gave his new married wife some counterfeit jewels, and as he was a pleasant droll, persuaded her that they were not only right but of an inestimable price; and what difference, I pray, to her, that was as well pleased and contented with glass and kept it as warily as if it had been a treasure? In the meantime the husband saved his money and had this advantage of her folly, that he obliged her as much as if he had bought them at a great rate. Or what difference, think you, between those in Plato's imaginary cave that stand gaping at the shadows and figures of things, so they please themselves and have no need to wish, and that wise man, who, being got loose from them, sees things truly as they are? Whereas that cobbler in Lucian if he might always have continued his golden dreams, he would never have desired any other happiness. So then there is no difference; or, if there be, the fools have the advantage: first, in that their happiness costs them least, that is to say, only some small persuasion; next, that they enjoy it in common. And the possession of no good can be delightful without a companion. For who does not know what a dearth there is of wise men, if yet any one be to be found? And though the Greeks for these so many ages have accounted upon seven only, yet so help me Hercules, do but examine them narrowly, and I'll be hanged if you find one half-witted fellow, nay or so much as one-quarter of a wise man, among them all.

For whereas among the many praises of Bacchus they reckon this the chief, that he washes away cares, and that too in an instant, do but sleep off his weak spirits, and they come on again, as we say, on horseback. But how much larger and more present is the benefit you receive by me, since, as it were with a perpetual drunkenness I fill your minds with mirth, fancies, and jollities, and that too without any trouble? Nor is there any man living whom I let be without it; whereas the gifts of the gods are scrambled, some to one and some to another. The sprightly delicious wine that drives away cares and leaves such a flavor behind it grows not everywhere. Beauty, the gift of Venus, happens to few; and to fewer gives Mercury eloquence. Hercules makes not everyone rich. Homer's Jupiter bestows not empire on all men. Mars oftentimes favors neither side. Many return sad from Apollo's oracle. Phoebus sometimes shoots a plague among us. Neptune drowns more than he saves: to say nothing of those mischievous gods, Plutoes, Ates, punishments, fevers, and the like, not gods but executioners. I am that only Folly that so readily and indifferently bestows my benefits on all. Nor do I look to be entreated, or am I subject to take pet, and require an expiatory sacrifice if some ceremony be omitted. Nor do I beat heaven and earth together if, when the rest of the gods are invited, I am passed by or not admitted to the stream of their sacrifices. For the rest of the gods are so curious in this point that such an omission may chance to spoil a man's business; and therefore one has as good even let them alone as worship them: just like some men, who are so hard to please, and withall so ready to do mischief, that 'tis better be a stranger than have any familiarity with them.

Desiderius Erasmus

But no man, you'll say, ever sacrificed to Folly or built me a temple. And troth, as I said before, I cannot but wonder at the ingratitude; yet because I am easily to be entreated, I take this also in good part, though truly I can scarce request it. For why should I require incense, wafers, a goat, or sow when all men pay me that worship everywhere which is so much approved even by our very divines? Unless perhaps I should envy Diana that her sacrifices are mingled with human blood. Then do I conceive myself most religiously worshipped when everywhere, as 'tis generally done, men embrace me in their minds, express me in their manners, and represent me in their lives, which worship of the saints is not so ordinary among Christians. How many are there that burn candles to the Virgin Mother, and that too at noonday when there's no need of them! But how few are there that study to imitate her in pureness of life, humility and love of heavenly things, which is the true worship and most acceptable to heaven! Besides why should I desire a temple when the whole world is my temple, and I'm deceived or 'tis a goodly one? Nor can I want priests but in a land where there are no men. Nor am I yet so foolish as to require statues or painted images, which do often obstruct my worship, since among the stupid and gross multitude those figures are worshipped for the saints themselves. And so it would fare with me, as it does with them that are turned out of doors by their substitutes. No, I have statues enough, and as many as there are men, everyone bearing my lively resemblance in his face, how unwilling so ever he be to the contrary. And therefore there is no reason why I should envy the rest of the gods if in particular places they have their particular worship, and that too on set days--as Phoebus at Rhodes; at Cyprus, Venus; at Argos, Juno; at Athens, Minerva; in Olympus, Jupiter; at Tarentum, Neptune; and near the Hellespont, Priapus--as long as the world in general performs me every day much better sacrifices.

Wherein notwithstanding if I shall seem to anyone to have spoken more boldly than truly, let us, if you please, look a little into the lives of men, and it will easily appear not only how much they owe to me, but how much they esteem me even from the highest to the lowest. And yet we will not run over the lives of everyone, for that would be too long, but only some few of the great ones, from whence we shall easily conjecture the rest. For to what purpose is it to say anything of the common people, who without dispute are wholly mine? For they abound everywhere with so many several sorts of folly, and are every day so busy in inventing new, that a thousand Democriti are too few for so general a laughter, though there were another Democritus to laugh at them too. 'Tis almost incredible what sport and pastime they daily make the gods; for though they set aside their sober forenoon hours to dispatch business and receive prayers, yet when they begin to be well whittled with nectar and cannot think of anything that's serious, they get them up into some part of heaven that has better prospect than other and thence look down upon the actions of men. Nor is there anything that pleases them better. Good, good! what an excellent sight it is! How many several hurly-burlies of fools! for I myself sometimes sit among those poetical gods.

Here's one desperately in love with a young wench, and the more she slights him the more outrageously he loves her. Another marries a woman's money, not herself. Another's jealousy keeps more eyes on her than Argos. Another becomes a mourner, and how foolishly he carries it! nay, hires others to bear him company to make it more ridiculous. Another weeps over his mother-in-law's grave. Another spends all he can rap and run on his belly, to be the more hungry after it. Another thinks there is no happiness but in sleep and idleness. Another turmoils himself about other men's business and neglects his own. Another thinks himself rich in taking up moneys and changing securities, as we say borrowing of Peter to pay Paul, and in a short time becomes bankrupt. Another starves himself to enrich his heir. Another for a small and uncertain gain exposes his life to the casualties of seas and winds, which yet no money can restore. Another had rather get riches by war than live peaceably at home. And some there are that think them easiest attained by courting old childless men with presents; and others again by making rich old women believe they love them; both which afford the gods most excellent pastime, to see them cheated by those persons they thought to have over-caught. But the most foolish and basest of all others are our merchants, to wit such as venture on everything be it never so dishonest, and manage it no better; who though they lie by no allowance, swear and forswear, steal, cozen, and cheat, yet shuffle themselves into the first rank, and all because they have gold rings on their fingers. Nor are they without their flattering friars that admire them and give them openly the title of honorable, in hopes, no doubt, to get some small snip of it themselves.

There are also a kind of Pythagoreans with whom all things are so common that if they get anything under their cloaks, they make no more scruple of carrying it away than if it were their own by inheritance. There are others too that are only rich in conceit, and while they fancy to themselves pleasant dreams, conceive that enough to make them happy. Some desire to be accounted wealthy abroad and are yet ready to starve at home. One makes what haste he can to set all going, and another rakes it together by right or wrong. This man is ever laboring for public honors, and another lies sleeping in a chimney corner. A great many undertake endless suits and outvie one another who shall most enrich the dilatory judge or corrupt advocate. One is all for innovations and another for some great he-knows-not-what. Another leaves his wife and children at home and goes to Jerusalem, Rome, or in pilgrimage to St. James's where he has no business. In short, if a man like Menippus of old could look down from the moon and behold those innumerable rufflings of mankind, he would think he saw a swarm of flies and gnats quarreling among themselves, fighting, laying traps for one another, snatching, playing, wantoning, growing up, falling, and dying. Nor is it to be believed what stir, what broils, this little creature raises, and yet in how short a time it comes to nothing itself; while sometimes war, other times pestilence, sweeps off many thousands of them together.

But let me be most foolish myself, and one whom Democritus may not only laugh at but flout, if I go one foot further in the discovery of the follies and madnesses of the common people. I'll betake me to them that carry the reputation of wise men and hunt after that golden bough, as says the proverb. Among whom the grammarians hold the first place, a generation of men than whom nothing would be more miserable, nothing more perplexed, nothing more hated of the gods, did not I allay the troubles of that pitiful profession with a certain kind of pleasant madness. For they are not only subject to those five curses with which Homer begins his Iliads, as says the Greek epigram, but six hundred; as being ever hungerstarved and slovens in their schools--schools, did I say? Nay, rather cloisters, bridewells, or slaughterhouses--grown old among a company of boys, deaf with their noise, and pined away with stench and nastiness. And yet by my courtesy it is that they think themselves the most excellent of all men, so greatly do they please themselves in frighting a company of fearful boys with a thundering voice and big looks, tormenting them with ferules, rods, and whips; and, laying about them without fear or wit, imitate the ass in the lion's skin. In the meantime all that nastiness seems absolute spruceness, that stench a perfume, and that miserable slavery a kingdom, and such too as they would not change their tyranny for Phalaris' or Dionysius' empire. Nor are they less happy in that new opinion they have taken up of being learned; for whereas most of them beat into boys, heads nothing but foolish toys, yet, you good gods! what Palemon, what Donatus, do they not scorn in comparison of themselves? And so, I know not by what tricks, they bring it about that to their boys' foolish mothers and dolt-headed fathers they pass for such as they fancy themselves. Add to this that other pleasure of theirs, that if any of them happen to find out who was Anchises' mother, or pick out of some worm-eaten manuscript a word not commonly known--as suppose it bubsequa for a cowherd, bovinator for a wrangler, manticulator for a cutpurse--or dig up the ruins of some ancient monument with the letters half eaten out; O Jupiter! what towerings! what triumphs! what commendations! as if they had conquered Africa or taken in Babylon.

But what of this when they give up and down their foolish insipid verses, and there wants not others that admire them as much? They believe presently that Virgil's soul is transmigrated into them! But nothing like this, when with mutual compliments they praise, admire, and claw one another. Whereas if another do but slip a word and one more quick-sighted than the rest discover it by accident, O Hercules! what uproars, what bickerings, what taunts, what invectives! If I lie, let me have the ill will of all the grammarians. I knew in my time one of many arts, a Grecian, a Latinist, a mathematician, a philosopher, a physician, a man master of them all, and sixty years of age, who, laying by all the rest, perplexed and tormented himself for above twenty years in the study of grammar, fully reckoning himself a prince if he might but live so long till he could certainly determine how the eight parts of speech were to be distinguished, which none of the Greeks or Latins had yet fully cleared: as if it were a matter to be decided by the sword if a man made an adverb of a conjunction. And for this cause is it that we have as many grammars as grammarians; nay more, forasmuch as my friend Aldus has given us above five, not passing by any kind of grammar, how barbarously or tediously soever compiled, which he has not turned over and examined; envying every man's attempts in this kind, how foolish so ever, and desperately concern'd for fear another should forestal him of his glory, and the labours of so many years perish. And now, whether had you rather call this Madness or Folly? It is no great matter to me whether, so long as ye confess it is by my means that a creature, otherwise the most miserable of all others, is rais'd to that height of felicity that he has no desire to change his condition with the King of Persia.

The Poets, I must confess, are not altogether so much beholding to me, though 'tis agreed of all hands they are of my partie too; because they are a free kind of people, not restrain'd or limited to any thing, and all their studies aim at nothing more than to tickle the ears of fools with meer trifles and ridiculous fables. And yet they are so bold upon 't, that you'll scarce believe how they not onely assure themselves of immortality and a life like the Gods, but promise it to others too. And to this order, before all others, Self-love and Flattery are more peculiarly appendant; nor am I worship by any sort of men with more plainness or greater constancy.

And then, for the Rhetoricians, though they now and then shuffle and cut with the Philosopher, yet that these two are of my faction also, though many other Arguments might be produc'd this clearly evinces exquisitely of Fooling. And so, who ever he were that writ of the Art of Rhetorick to Herennius, he reckons Folly as a species of wit. And Quintilian, the Soveraign of this Order, has a Chapter touching Laughter more prolixe than an Iliad. In fine, they attribute so much to Folly, that what many times cannot be clear'd with the best Arguments, is yet now and then put off with a jest: unless, perhaps you'll say, 'tis no part of Folly to provoke laughter, and that artificially.

Desiderius Erasmus

Of the same batch also are they that hunt after immortality of Fame by setting out Books. Of whom, though all of 'em arre endebted to me, yet in the first place are they that nothing but daub Paper with their empty Toyes. For they that write learnedly to the understanding of a few Scholers, and refuse not to stand the test of a Persius or Laelius, seem to me rather to be pitied than happy, as persons that are ever tormenting themselves; adding, changing, putting in, blotting out, revising, reprinting, showing it to friends, and nine years in correcting, yet never fully satisfied; at so great a rate do they purchase this vain reward, to wit, praise, and that too of a very few, with so many watchings, so much sweat, so much vexation and loss of sleep, the most precious of all things. Add to this the waste of health, spoil of complexion, weakness of eyes or rather blindness, poverty, envy, abstinence from pleasure, over-hasty old age, untimely death, and the like; so highly does this wise man value the approbation of one or two blear-eyed fellows. But how much happier is this my writer's dotage who never studies for anything but puts in writing whatever he pleases or what comes first in his head, though it be but his dreams; and all this with small waste of paper, as well knowing that the vainer those trifles are, the higher esteem they will have with the greater number, that is to say all the fools and unlearned. And what matter is it to slight those few learned if yet they ever read them? Or of what authority will the censure of so few wise men be against so great a cloud of gainsayers?

But they are the wiser that put out other men's works for their own, and transfer that glory which others with great pains have obtained to themselves; relying on this, that they conceive, though it should so happen that their theft be never so plainly detected, that yet they should enjoy the pleasure of it for the present. And 'tis worth one's while to consider how they please themselves when they are applauded by the common people, pointed at in a crowd, "This is that excellent person;" lie on booksellers' stalls; and in the top of every page have three hard words read, but chiefly exotic and next degree to conjuring; which, by the immortal gods! what are they but mere words? And again, if you consider the world, by how few understood, and praised by fewer! for even among the unlearned there are different palates. Or what is it that their own very names are often counterfeit or borrowed from some books of the ancients? When one styles himself Telemachus, another Sthenelus, a third Laertes, a fourth Polycrates, a fifth Thrasymachus. So that there is no difference whether they title their books with the "Tale of a Tub," or, according to the philosophers, by alpha, beta.

But the most pleasant of all is to see them praise one another with reciprocal epistles, verses, and encomiums; fools their fellow fools, and dunces their brother dunces. This, in the other's opinion, is an absolute Alcaeus; and the other, in his, a very Callimachus. He looks upon Tully as nothing to the other, and the other again pronounces him more learned than Plato. And sometimes too they pick out their antagonist and think to raise themselves a fame by writing one against the other; while the giddy multitude are so long divided to whether of the two they shall determine the victory, till each goes off conqueror, and, as if he had done some great action, fancies himself a triumph. And now wise men laugh at these things as foolish, as indeed they are. Who denies it? Yet in the meantime, such is my kindness to them, they live a merry life and would not change their imaginary triumphs, no, not with the Scipioes. While yet those learned men, though they laugh their fill and reap the benefit of the other's folly, cannot without ingratitude deny but that even they too are not a little beholding to me themselves.

And among them our advocates challenge the first place, nor is there any sort of people that please themselves like them: for while they daily roll Sisyphus his stone, and quote you a thousand cases, as it were, in a breath no matter how little to the purpose, and heap glosses upon glosses, and opinions on the neck of opinions, they bring it at last to this pass, that that study of all other seems the most difficult. Add to these our logicians and sophists, a generation of men more prattling than an echo and the worst of them able to outchat a hundred of the best picked gossips. And yet their condition would be much better were they only full of words and not so given to scolding that they most obstinately hack and hew one another about a matter of nothing and make such a sputter about terms and words till they have quite lost the sense. And yet they are so happy in the good opinion of themselves that as soon as they are furnished with two or three syllogisms, they dare boldly enter the lists against any man upon any point, as not doubting but to run him down with noise, though the opponent were another Stentor.

And next these come our philosophers, so much reverenced for their furred gowns and starched beards that they look upon themselves as the only wise men and all others as shadows. And yet how pleasantly do they dote while they frame in their heads innumerable worlds; measure out the sun, the moon, the stars, nay and heaven itself, as it were, with a pair of compasses; lay down the causes of lightning, winds, eclipses, and other the like inexplicable matters; and all this too without the least doubting, as if they were Nature's secretaries, or dropped down among us from the council of the gods; while in the meantime Nature laughs at them and all their blind conjectures. For that they know nothing, even this is a sufficient argument, that they don't agree among themselves and so are incomprehensible touching every particular. These, though they have not the least degree of knowledge, profess yet that they have mastered all; nay, though they neither know themselves, nor perceive a ditch or block that lies in their way, for that perhaps most of them are half blind, or their wits a wool-gathering, yet give out that they have discovered ideas, universalities, separated forms, first matters, quiddities, haecceities, formalities, and the like stuff; things so thin and bodiless that I believe even Lynceus himself was not able to perceive them. But then chiefly do they disdain the unhallowed crowd as often as with their triangles, quadrangles, circles, and the like mathematical devices, more confounded than a labyrinth, and letters disposed one against the other, as it were in battle array, they cast a mist before the eyes of the ignorant. Nor is there wanting of this kind some that pretend to foretell things by the stars and make promises of miracles beyond all things of soothsaying, and are so fortunate as to meet with people that believe them.

But perhaps I had better pass over our divines in silence and not stir this pool or touch this fair but unsavory plant, as a kind of men that are supercilious beyond comparison, and to that too, implacable; lest setting them about my ears, they attack me by troops and force me to a recantation sermon, which if I refuse, they straight pronounce me a heretic. For this is the thunderbolt with which they fright those whom they are resolved not to favor. And truly, though there are few others that less willingly acknowledge the kindnesses I have done them, yet even these too stand fast bound to me upon no ordinary accounts; while being happy in their own opinion, and as if they dwelt in the third heaven, they look with haughtiness on all others as poor creeping things and could almost find in their hearts to pity them; while hedged in with so many magisterial definitions, conclusions, corollaries, propositions explicit and implicit, they abound with so many starting-holes that Vulcan's net cannot hold them so fast, but they'll slip through with their distinctions, with which they so easily cut all knots asunder that a hatchet could not have done it better, so plentiful are they in their new-found words and prodigious terms. Besides, while they explicate the most hidden mysteries according to their own fancy--as how the world was first made; how original sin is derived to posterity; in what manner, how much room, and how long time Christ lay in the Virgin's womb; how accidents subsist in the Eucharist without their subject.

But these are common and threadbare; these are worthy of our great and illuminated divines, as the world calls them! At these, if ever they fall athwart them, they prick up--as whether there was any instant of time in the generation of the Second Person; whether there be more than one filiation in Christ; whether it be a possible proposition that God the Father hates the Son; or whether it was possible that Christ could have taken upon Him the likeness of a woman, or of the devil, or of an ass, or of a stone, or of a gourd; and then how that gourd should have preached, wrought miracles, or been hung on the cross; and what Peter had consecrated if he had administered the Sacrament at what time the body of Christ hung upon the cross; or whether at the same time he might be said to be man; whether after the Resurrection there will be any eating and drinking, since we are so much afraid of hunger and thirst in this world. There are infinite of these subtle trifles, and others more subtle than these, of notions, relations, instants, formalities, quiddities, haecceities, which no one can perceive without a Lynceus whose eyes could look through a stone wall and discover those things through the thickest darkness that never were.

Add to this those their other determinations, and those too so contrary to common opinion that those oracles of the Stoics, which they call paradoxes, seem in comparison of these but blockish and idle--as 'tis a lesser crime to kill a thousand men than to set a stitch on a poor man's shoe on the Sabbath day; and that a man should rather choose that the whole world with all food and raiment, as they say, should perish, than tell a lie, though never so inconsiderable. And these most subtle subtleties are rendered yet more subtle by the several methods of so many Schoolmen, that one might sooner wind himself out of a labyrinth than the entanglements of the realists, nominalists, Thomists, Albertists, Occamists, Scotists. Nor have I named all the several sects, but only some of the chief; in all which there is so much doctrine and so much difficulty that I may well conceive the apostles, had they been to deal with these new kind of divines, had needed to have prayed in aid of some other spirit.

Paul knew what faith was, and yet when he said, "Faith is the substance of things hoped for, and the evidence of things not seen," he did not define it doctor-like. And as he understood charity well himself, so he did as illogically divide and define it to others in his first Epistle to the Corinthians, Chapter the thirteenth. And devoutly, no doubt, did the apostles consecrate the Eucharist; yet, had they been asked the question touching the "terminus a quo," and the "terminus ad quem" of transubstantiation; of the manner how the same body can be in several places at one and the same time; of the difference the body of Christ has in heaven from that of the cross, or this in the Sacrament; in what point of time transubstantiation is, whereas prayer, by means of which it is, as being a discrete quantity, is transient; they would not, I conceive, have answered with the same subtlety as the Scotists dispute and define it. They knew the mother of Jesus, but which of them has so philosophically demonstrated how she was preserved from original sin as have done our divines? Peter received the keys, and from Him too that would not have trusted them with a person unworthy; yet whether he had understanding or no, I know not, for certainly he never attained to that subtlety to determine how he could have the key of knowledge that had no knowledge himself. They baptized far and near, and yet taught nowhere what was the formal, material, efficient, and final cause of baptism, nor made the least mention of delible and indelible characters. They worshipped, 'tis true, but in spirit, following herein no other than that of the Gospel, "God is a Spirit, and they that worship, must worship him in spirit and truth;" yet it does not appear it was at that time revealed to them that an image sketched on the wall with a coal was to be worshipped with the same worship as Christ Himself, if at least the two forefingers be stretched out, the hair long and uncut, and have three rays about the crown of the head. For who can conceive these things, unless he has spent at least six and thirty years in the philosophical and supercelestial whims of Aristotle and the Schoolmen?

In like manner, the apostles press to us grace; but which of them distinguishes between free grace and grace that makes a man acceptable? They exhort us to good works, and yet determine not what is the work working, and what a resting in the work done. They incite us to charity, and yet make no difference between charity infused and charity wrought in us by our own endeavors. Nor do they declare whether it be an accident or a substance, a thing created or uncreated. They detest and abominate sin, but let me not live if they could define according to art what that is which we call sin, unless perhaps they were inspired by the spirit of the Scotists. Nor can I be brought to believe that Paul, by whose learning you may judge the rest, would have so often condemned questions, disputes, genealogies, and, as himself calls them, "strifes of words," if he had thoroughly understood those subtleties, especially when all the debates and controversies of those times were rude and blockish in comparison of the more than Chrysippean subtleties of our masters. Although yet the gentlemen are so modest that if they meet with anything written by the apostles not so smooth and even as might be expected from a master, they do not presently condemn it but handsomely bend it to their own purpose, so great respect and honor do they give, partly to antiquity and partly to the name of apostle. And truly 'twas a kind of injustice to require so great things of them that never heard the least word from their masters concerning it. And so if the like happen in Chrysostom, Basil, Jerome, they think it enough to say they are not obliged by it.

The apostles also confuted the heathen philosophers and Jews, a people than whom none more obstinate, but rather by their good lives and miracles than by syllogisms: and yet there was scarce one among them that was capable of understanding the least "quodlibet" of the Scotists. But now, where is that heathen or heretic that must not presently stoop to such wire-drawn subtleties, unless he be so thickskulled that he can't apprehend them, or so impudent as to hiss them down, or, being furnished with the same tricks, be able to make his party good with them? As if a man should set a conjurer on work against a conjurer, or fight with one hallowed sword against another, which would prove no other than a work to no purpose. For my own part I conceive the Christians would do much better if instead of those dull troops and companies of soldiers with which they have managed their war with such doubtful success, they would send the bawling Scotists, the most obstinate Occamists, and invincible Albertists to war against the Turks and Saracens; and they would see, I guess, a most pleasant combat and such a victory as was never before. For who is so faint whom their devices will not enliven? who so stupid whom such spurs can't quicken? or who so quicksighted before whose eyes they can't cast a mist?

But you'll say, I jest. Nor are you without cause, since even among divines themselves there are some that have learned better and are ready to turn their stomachs at those foolish subtleties of the others. There are some that detest them as a kind of sacrilege and count it the height of impiety to speak so irreverently of such hidden things, rather to be adored than explicated; to dispute of them with such profane and heathenish niceties; to define them so arrogantly and pollute the majesty of divinity with such pithless and sordid terms and opinions. Meantime the others please, nay hug themselves in their happiness, and are so taken up with these pleasant trifles that they have not so much leisure as to cast the least eye on the Gospel or St. Paul's epistles. And while they play the fool at this rate in their schools, they make account the universal church would otherwise perish, unless, as the poets fancied of Atlas that he supported heaven with his shoulders, they underpropped the other with their syllogistical buttresses. And how great a happiness is this, think you? while, as if Holy Writ were a nose of wax, they fashion and refashion it according to their pleasure; while they require that their own conclusions, subscribed by two or three Schoolmen, be accounted greater than Solon's laws and preferred before the papal decretals; while, as censors of the world, they force everyone to a recantation that differs but a hair's breadth from the least of their explicit or implicit determinations. And those too they pronounce like oracles. This proposition is scandalous; this irreverent; this has a smack of heresy; this no very good sound: so that neither baptism, nor the Gospel, nor Paul, nor Peter, nor St. Jerome, nor St. Augustine, no nor most Aristotelian Thomas himself can make a man a Christian, without these bachelors too be pleased to give him his grace. And the like in their subtlety in judging; for who would think he were no Christian that should say these two speeches "matula putes" and "matula putet," or "ollae fervere" and "ollam fervere" were not both good Latin, unless their wisdoms had taught us the contrary? who had delivered the church from such mists of error, which yet no one ever met with, had they not come out with some university seal for it? And are they not most happy while they do these things?

Then for what concerns hell, how exactly they describe everything, as if they had been conversant in that commonwealth most part of their time! Again, how do they frame in their fancy new orbs, adding to those we have already an eighth! a goodly one, no doubt, and spacious enough, lest perhaps their happy souls might lack room to walk in, entertain their friends, and now and then play at football.

Against War and In Praise of Folly
And with these and a thousand the like fopperies their heads are so full stuffed and stretched that I believe Jupiter's brain was not near so big when, being in labor with Pallas, he was beholding to the midwifery of Vulcan's ax. And therefore you must not wonder if in their public disputes they are so bound about the head, lest otherwise perhaps their brains might leap out. Nay, I have sometimes laughed myself to see them so tower in their own opinion when they speak most barbarously; and when they humh and hawh so pitifully that none but one of their own tribe can understand them, they call it heights which the vulgar can't reach; for they say 'tis beneath the dignity of divine mysteries to be cramped and tied up to the narrow rules of grammarians: from whence we may conjecture the great prerogative of divines, if they only have the privilege of speaking corruptly, in which yet every cobbler thinks himself concerned for his share. Lastly, they look upon themselves as somewhat more than men as often as they are devoutly saluted by the name of "Our Masters," in which they fancy there lies as much as in the Jews' "Jehovah;" and therefore they reckon it a crime if "Magister Noster" be written other than in capital letters; and if anyone should preposterously say "Noster Magister," he has at once overturned the whole body of divinity.

And next these come those that commonly call themselves the religious and monks, most false in both titles, when both a great part of them are farthest from religion, and no men swarm thicker in all places than themselves. Nor can I think of anything that could be more miserable did not I support them so many several ways. For whereas all men detest them to that height, that they take it for ill luck to meet one of them by chance, yet such is their happiness that they flatter themselves. For first, they reckon it one of the main points of piety if they are so illiterate that they can't so much as read. And then when they run over their offices, which they carry about them, rather by tale than understanding, they believe the gods more than ordinarily pleased with their braying. And some there are among them that put off their trumperies at vast rates, yet rove up and down for the bread they eat; nay, there is scarce an inn, wagon, or ship into which they intrude not, to the no small damage of the commonwealth of beggars. And yet, like pleasant fellows, with all this vileness, ignorance, rudeness, and impudence, they represent to us, for so they call it, the lives of the apostles. Yet what is more pleasant than that they do all things by rule and, as it were, a kind of mathematics, the least swerving from which were a crime beyond forgiveness--as how many knots their shoes must be tied with, of what color everything is, what distinction of habits, of what stuff made, how many straws broad their girdles and of what fashion, how many bushels wide their cowl, how many fingers long their hair, and how many hours sleep; which exact equality, how disproportionate it is, among such variety of bodies and tempers, who is there that does not perceive it? And yet by reason of these fooleries they not only set slight by others, but each different order, men otherwise professing apostolical charity, despise one another, and for the different wearing of a habit, or that 'tis of darker color, they put all things in combustion. And among these there are some so rigidly religious that their upper garment is haircloth, their inner of the finest linen; and, on the contrary, others wear linen without and hair next their skins. Others, again, are as afraid to touch money as poison, and yet neither forbear wine nor dallying with women. In a word, 'tis their only care that none of them come near one another in their manner of living, nor do they endeavor how they may be like Christ, but how they may differ among themselves.

And another great happiness they conceive in their names, while they call themselves Cordiliers, and among these too, some are Colletes, some Minors, some Minims, some Crossed; and again, these are Benedictines, those Bernardines; these Carmelites, those Augustines: these Williamites, and those Jacobines; as if it were not worth the while to be called Christians. And of these, a great part build so much on their ceremonies and petty traditions of men that they think one heaven is too poor a reward for so great merit, little dreaming that the time will come when Christ, not regarding any of these trifles, will call them to account for His precept of charity. One shall show you a large trough full of all kinds of fish; another tumble you out so many bushels of prayers; another reckon you so many myriads of fasts, and fetch them up again in one dinner by eating till he cracks again; another produces more bundles of ceremonies than seven of the stoutest ships would be able to carry; another brags he has not touched a penny these three score years without two pair of gloves at least upon his hands; another wears a cowl so lined with grease that the poorest tarpaulin would not stoop to take it up; another will tell you he has lived these fifty-five years like a sponge, continually fastened to the same place; another is grown hoarse with his daily chanting; another has contracted a lethargy by his solitary living; and another the palsy in his tongue for want of speaking. But Christ, interrupting them in their vanities, which otherwise were endless, will ask them, "Whence this new kind of Jews? I acknowledge one commandment, which is truly mine, of which alone I hear nothing. I promised, 'tis true, my Father's heritage, and that without parables, not to cowls, odd prayers, and fastings, but to the duties of faith and charity. Nor can I acknowledge them that least acknowledge their faults. They that would seem holier than myself, let them if they like possess to themselves those three hundred sixty-five heavens of Basilides the heretic's invention, or command them whose foolish traditions they have preferred before my precepts to erect them a new one." When they shall hear these things and see common ordinary persons preferred before them, with what countenance, think you, will they behold one another? In the meantime they are happy in their hopes, and for this also they are beholding to me.

And yet these kind of people, though they are as it were of another commonwealth, no man dares despise, especially those begging friars, because they are privy to all men's secrets by means of confessions, as they call them. Which yet were no less than treason to discover, unless, being got drunk, they have a mind to be pleasant, and then all comes out, that is to say by hints and conjectures but suppressing the names. But if anyone should anger these wasps, they'll sufficiently revenge themselves in their public sermons and so point out their enemy by circumlocutions that there's no one but understands whom 'tis they mean, unless he understand nothing at all; nor will they give over their barking till you throw the dogs a bone. And now tell me, what juggler or mountebank you had rather behold than hear them rhetorically play the fool in their preachments, and yet most sweetly imitating what rhetoricians have written touching the art of good speaking? Good God! what several postures they have! How they shift their voice, sing out their words, skip up and down, and are ever and anon making such new faces that they confound all things with noise! And yet this knack of theirs is no less a mystery that runs in succession from one brother to another; which though it be not lawful for me to know, however I'll venture at it by conjectures. And first they invoke whatever they have scraped from the poets; and in the next place, if they are to discourse of charity, they take their rise from the river Nilus; or to set out the mystery of the cross, from bell and the dragon; or to dispute of fasting, from the twelve signs of the zodiac; or, being to preach of faith, ground their matter on the square of a circle.

I have heard myself one, and he no small fool--I was mistaken, I would have said scholar--that being in a famous assembly explaining the mystery of the Trinity, that he might both let them see his learning was not ordinary and withal satisfy some theological ears, he took a new way, to wit from the letters, syllables, and the word itself; then from the coherence of the nominative case and the verb, and the adjective and substantive: and while most of the audience wondered, and some of them muttered that of Horace, "What does all this trumpery drive at?" at last he brought the matter to this head, that he would demonstrate that the mystery of the Trinity was so clearly expressed in the very rudiments of grammar that the best mathematician could not chalk it out more plainly. And in this discourse did this most superlative theologian beat his brains for eight whole months that at this hour he's as blind as a beetle, to wit, all the sight of his eyes being run into the sharpness of his wit. But for all that he thinks nothing of his blindness, rather taking the same for too cheap a price of such a glory as he won thereby.

And besides him I met with another, some eighty years of age, and such a divine that you'd have sworn Scotus himself was revived in him. He, being upon the point of unfolding the mystery of the name Jesus, did with wonderful subtlety demonstrate that there lay hidden in those letters whatever could be said of him; for that it was only declined with three cases, he said, it was a manifest token of the Divine Trinity; and then, that the first ended in S, the second in M, the third in U, there was in it an ineffable mystery, to wit, those three letters declaring to us that he was the beginning, middle, and end (summum, medium, et ultimum) of all. Nay, the mystery was yet more abstruse; for he so mathematically split the word Jesus into two equal parts that he left the middle letter by itself, and then told us that that letter in Hebrew was schin or sin, and that sin in the Scotch tongue, as he remembered, signified as much as sin; from whence he gathered that it was Jesus that took away the sins of the world. At which new exposition the audience were so wonderfully intent and struck with admiration, especially the theologians, that there wanted little but that Niobe-like they had been turned to stones; whereas the like had almost happened to me, as befell the Priapus in Horace. And not without cause, for when were the Grecian Demosthenes or Roman Cicero ever guilty of the like? They thought that introduction faulty that was wide of the matter, as if it were not the way of carters and swineherds that have no more wit than God sent them. But these learned men think their preamble, for so they call it, then chiefly rhetorical when it has least coherence with the rest of the argument, that the admiring audience may in the meanwhile whisper to themselves, "What will he be at now?" In the third place, they bring in instead of narration some texts of Scripture, but handle them cursorily, and as it were by the bye, when yet it is the only thing they should have insisted on. And fourthly, as it were changing a part in the play, they bolt out with some question in divinity, and many times relating neither to earth nor heaven, and this they look upon as a piece of art. Here they erect their theological crests and beat into the people's ears those magnificent titles of illustrious doctors, subtle doctors, most subtle doctors, seraphic doctors, cherubic doctors, holy doctors, unquestionable doctors, and the like; and then throw abroad among the ignorant people syllogisms, majors, minors, conclusions, corollaries, suppositions, and those so weak and foolish that they are below pedantry. There remains yet the fifth act in which one would think they should show their mastery. And here they bring in some foolish insipid fable out of Speculum Historiae or Gesta Romanorum and expound it allegorically, tropologically, and anagogically. And after this manner do they and their chimera, and such as Horace despaired of compassing when he wrote "Humano capiti," etc.

But they have heard from somebody, I know not whom, that the beginning of a speech should be sober and grave and least given to noise. And therefore they begin theirs at that rate they can scarce hear themselves, as if it were not matter whether anyone understood them. They have learned somewhere that to move the affections a louder voice is requisite. Whereupon they that otherwise would speak like a mouse in a cheese start out of a sudden into a downright fury, even there too, where there's the least need of it. A man would swear they were past the power of hellebore, so little do they consider where 'tis they run out. Again, because they have heard that as a speech comes up to something, a man should press it more earnestly, they, however they begin, use a strange contention of voice in every part, though the matter itself be never so flat, and end in that manner as if they'd run themselves out of breath. Lastly, they have learned that among rhetoricians there is some mention of laughter, and therefore they study to prick in a jest here and there; but, O Venus! so void of wit and so little to the purpose that it may be truly called an ass's playing on the harp. And sometimes also they use somewhat of a sting, but so nevertheless that they rather tickle than wound; nor do they ever more truly flatter than when they would seem to use the greatest freedom of speech. Lastly, such is their whole action that a man would swear they had learned it from our common tumblers, though yet they come short of them in every respect. However, they are both so like that no man will dispute but that either these learned their rhetoric from them, or they theirs from these. And yet they light on some that, when they hear them, conceive they hear very Demosthenes and Ciceroes: of which sort chiefly are our merchants and women, whose ears only they endeavor to please, because as to the first, if they stroke them handsomely, some part or other of their ill-gotten goods is wont to fall to their share. And the women, though for many other things they favor this order, this is not the least, that they commit to their breasts whatever discontents they have against their husbands. And now, I conceive me, you see how much this kind of people are beholding to me, that with their petty ceremonies, ridiculous trifles, and noise exercise a kind of tyranny among mankind, believing themselves very Pauls and Anthonies.

But I willingly give over these stage-players that are such ingrateful dissemblers of the courtesies I have done them and such impudent pretenders to religion which they haven't. And now I have a mind to give some small touches of princes and courts, of whom I am had in reverence, aboveboard and, as it becomes gentlemen, frankly. And truly, if they had the least proportion of sound judgment, what life were more unpleasant than theirs, or so much to be avoided? For whoever did but truly weigh with himself how great a burden lies upon his shoulders that would truly discharge the duty of a prince, he would not think it worth his while to make his way to a crown by perjury and parricide. He would consider that he that takes a scepter in his hand should manage the public, not his private, interest; study nothing but the common good; and not in the least go contrary to those laws whereof himself is both the author and exactor: that he is to take an account of the good or evil administration of all his magistrates and subordinate officers; that, though he is but one, all men's eyes are upon him, and in his power it is, either like a good planet to give life and safety to mankind by his harmless influence, or like a fatal comet to send mischief and destruction; that the vices of other men are not alike felt, nor so generally communicated; and that a prince stands in that place that his least deviation from the rule of honesty and honor reaches farther than himself and opens a gap to many men's ruin. Besides, that the fortune of princes has many things attending it that are but too apt to train them out of the way, as pleasure, liberty, flattery, excess; for which cause he should the more diligently endeavor and set a watch over himself, lest perhaps he be led aside and fail in his duty. Lastly, to say nothing of treasons, ill will, and such other mischiefs he's in jeopardy of, that that True King is over his head, who in a short time will call him to account for every the least trespass, and that so much the more severely by how much more mighty was the empire committed to his charge. These and the like if a prince should duly weigh, and weigh it he would if he were wise, he would neither be able to sleep nor take any hearty repast.

But now by my courtesy they leave all this care to the gods and are only taken up with themselves, not admitting anyone to their ear but such as know how to speak pleasant things and not trouble them with business. They believe they have discharged all the duty of a prince if they hunt every day, keep a stable of fine horses, sell dignities and commanderies, and invent new ways of draining the citizens' purses and bringing it into their own exchequer; but under such dainty new-found names that though the thing be most unjust in itself, it carries yet some face of equity; adding to this some little sweetening that whatever happens, they may be secure of the common people. And now suppose someone, such as they sometimes are, a man ignorant of laws, little less than an enemy to the public good, and minding nothing but his own, given up to pleasure, a hater of learning, liberty, and justice, studying nothing less than the public safety, but measuring everything by his own will and profit; and then put on him a golden chain that declares the accord of all virtues linked one to another; a crown set with diamonds, that should put him in mind how he ought to excel all others in heroic virtues; besides a scepter, the emblem of justice and an untainted heart; and lastly, a purple robe, a badge of that charity he owes the commonwealth. All which if a prince should compare them with his own life, he would, I believe, be clearly ashamed of his bravery, and be afraid lest some or other gibing expounder turn all this tragical furniture into a ridiculous laughingstock.

And as to the court lords, what should I mention them? than most of whom though there be nothing more indebted, more servile, more witless, more contemptible, yet they would seem as they were the most excellent of all others. And yet in this only thing no men more modest, in that they are contented to wear about them gold, jewels, purple, and those other marks of virtue and wisdom; but for the study of the things themselves, they remit it to others, thinking it happiness enough for them that they can call the king master, have learned the cringe a la mode, know when and where to use those titles of Your Grace, My Lord, Your Magnificence; in a word that they are past all shame and can flatter pleasantly. For these are the arts that speak a man truly noble and an exact courtier. But if you look into their manner of life you'll find them mere sots, as debauched as Penelope's wooers; you know the other part of the verse, which the echo will better tell you than I can. They sleep till noon and have their mercenary Levite come to their bedside, where he chops over his matins before they are half up. Then to breakfast, which is scarce done but dinner stays for them. From thence they go to dice, tables, cards, or entertain themselves with jesters, fools, gambols, and horse tricks. In the meantime they have one or two beverages, and then supper, and after that a banquet, and 'twere well, by Jupiter, there were no more than one. And in this manner do their hours, days, months, years, age slide away without the least irksomeness. Nay, I have sometimes gone away many inches fatter, to see them speak big words; while each of the ladies believes herself so much nearer to the gods by how much the longer train she trails after her; while one nobleman edges out another, that he may get the nearer to Jupiter himself; and everyone of them pleases himself the more by how much more massive is the chain he swags on his shoulders, as if he meant to show his strength as well as his wealth.

    Nor are princes by themselves in their manner of life, since popes, cardinals, and bishops have so diligently followed their steps that they've almost got the start of them. For if any of them would consider what their alb should put them in mind of, to wit a blameless life; what is meant by their forked miters, whose each point is held in by the same knot, we'll suppose it a perfect knowledge of the Old and New Testaments; what those gloves on their hands, but a sincere administration of the Sacraments, and free from all touch of worldly business; what their crosier, but a careful looking after the flock committed to their charge; what the cross born before them, but victory over all earthly affections-- these, I say, and many of the like kind should anyone truly consider, would he not live a sad and troublesome life? Whereas now they do well enough while they feed themselves only, and for the care of their flock either put it over to Christ or lay it all on their suffragans, as they call them, or some poor vicars. Nor do they so much as remember their name, or what the word bishop signifies, to wit, labor, care, and trouble. But in racking to gather money they truly act the part of bishops, and herein acquit themselves to be no blind seers.

    In like manner cardinals, if they thought themselves the successors of the apostles, they would likewise imagine that the same things the other did are required of them, and that they are not lords but dispensers of spiritual things of which they must shortly give an exact account. But if they also would a little philosophize on their habit and think with themselves what's the meaning of their linen rochet, is it not a remarkable and singular integrity of life? What that inner purple; is it not an earnest and fervent love of God? Or what that outward, whose loose plaits and long train fall round his Reverence's mule and are large enough to cover a camel; is it not charity that spreads itself so wide to the succor of all men? that is, to instruct, exhort, comfort, reprehend, admonish, compose wars, resist wicked princes, and willingly expend not only their wealth but their very lives for the flock of Christ: though yet what need at all of wealth to them that supply the room of the poor apostles? these things, I say, did they but duly consider, they would not be so ambitious of that dignity; or, if they were, they would willingly leave it and live a laborious, careful life, such as was that of the ancient apostles.

    And for popes, that supply the place of Christ, if they should endeavor to imitate His life, to wit His poverty, labor, doctrine, cross, and contempt of life, or should they consider what the name pope, that is father, or holiness, imports, who would live more disconsolate than themselves? or who would purchase that chair with all his substance? or defend it, so purchased, with swords, poisons, and all force imaginable? so great a profit would the access of wisdom deprive him of--wisdom did I say? nay, the least corn of that salt which Christ speaks of: so much wealth, so much honor, so much riches, so many victories, so many offices, so many dispensations, so much tribute, so many pardons; such horses, such mules, such guards, and so much pleasure would it lose them. You see how much I have comprehended in a little: instead of which it would bring in watchings, fastings, tears, prayers, sermons, good endeavors, sighs, and a thousand the like troublesome exercises. Nor is this least considerable: so many scribes, so many copying clerks, so many notaries, so many advocates, so many promoters, so many secretaries, so many muleteers, so many grooms, so many bankers: in short, that vast multitude of men that overcharge the Roman See--I mistook, I meant honor--might beg their bread.

    A most inhuman and economical thing, and more to be execrated, that those great princes of the Church and true lights of the world should be reduced to a staff and a wallet. Whereas now, if there be anything that requires their pains, they leave that to Peter and Paul that have leisure enough; but if there be anything of honor or pleasure, they take that to themselves. By which means it is, yet by my courtesy, that scarce any kind of men live more voluptuously or with less trouble; as believing that Christ will be well enough pleased if in their mystical and almost mimical pontificality, ceremonies, titles of holiness and the like, and blessing and cursing, they play the parts of bishops. To work miracles is old and antiquated, and not in fashion now; to instruct the people, troublesome; to interpret the Scripture, pedantic; to pray, a sign one has little else to do; to shed tears, silly and womanish; to be poor, base; to be vanquished, dishonorable and little becoming him that scarce admits even kings to kiss his slipper; and lastly, to die, uncouth; and to be stretched on a cross, infamous.

Theirs are only those weapons and sweet blessings which Paul mentions, and of these truly they are bountiful enough: as interdictions, hangings, heavy burdens, reproofs, anathemas, executions in effigy, and that terrible thunderbolt of excommunication, with the very sight of which they sink men's souls beneath the bottom of hell: which yet these most holy fathers in Christ and His vicars hurl with more fierceness against none than against such as, by the instigation of the devil, attempt to lessen or rob them of Peter's patrimony. When, though those words in the Gospel, "We have left all, and followed Thee," were his, yet they call his patrimony lands, cities, tribute, imposts, riches; for which, being enflamed with the love of Christ, they contend with fire and sword, and not without loss of much Christian blood, and believe they have then most apostolically defended the Church, the spouse of Christ, when the enemy, as they call them, are valiantly routed. As if the Church had any deadlier enemies than wicked prelates, who not only suffer Christ to run out of request for want of preaching him, but hinder his spreading by their multitudes of laws merely contrived for their own profit, corrupt him by their forced expositions, and murder him by the evil example of their pestilent life.

Nay, further, whereas the Church of Christ was founded in blood, confirmed by blood, and augmented by blood, now, as if Christ, who after his wonted manner defends his people, were lost, they govern all by the sword. And whereas war is so savage a thing that it rather befits beasts than men, so outrageous that the very poets feigned it came from the Furies, so pestilent that it corrupts all men's manners, so unjust that it is best executed by the worst of men, so wicked that it has no agreement with Christ; and yet, omitting all the other, they make this their only business. Here you'll see decrepit old fellows acting the parts of young men, neither troubled at their costs, nor wearied with their labors, nor discouraged at anything, so they may have the liberty of turning laws, religion, peace, and all things else quite topsy-turvy. Nor are they destitute of their learned flatterers that call that palpable madness zeal, piety, and valor, having found out a new way by which a man may kill his brother without the least breach of that charity which, by the command of Christ, one Christian owes another. And here, in truth, I'm a little at a stand whether the ecclesiastical German electors gave them this example, or rather took it from them; who, laying aside their habit, benedictions, and all the like ceremonies, so act the part of commanders that they think it a mean thing, and least beseeming a bishop, to show the least courage to Godward unless it be in a battle.

And as to the common herd of priests, they account it a crime to degenerate from the sanctity of their prelates. Heidah! How soldier-like they bustle about the jus divinum of titles, and how quicksighted they are to pick the least thing out of the writings of the ancients wherewith they may fright the common people and convince them, if possible, that more than a tenth is due! Yet in the meantime it least comes in their heads how many things are everywhere extant concerning that duty which they owe the people. Nor does their shorn crown in the least admonish them that a priest should be free from all worldly desires and think of nothing but heavenly things. Whereas on the contrary, these jolly fellows say they have sufficiently discharged their offices if they but anyhow mumble over a few odd prayers, which, so help me, Hercules! I wonder if any god either hear or understand, since they do neither themselves, especially when they thunder them out in that manner they are wont. But this they have in common with those of the heathens, that they are vigilant enough to the harvest of their profit, nor is there any of them that is not better read in those laws than the Scripture. Whereas if there be anything burdensome, they prudently lay that on other men's shoulders and shift it from one to the other, as men toss a ball from hand to hand, following herein the example of lay princes who commit the government of their kingdoms to their grand ministers, and they again to others, and leave all study of piety to the common people. In like manner the common people put it over to those they call ecclesiastics, as if themselves were no part of the Church, or that their vow in baptism had lost its obligation. Again, the priests that call themselves secular, as if they were initiated to the world, not to Christ, lay the burden on the regulars; the regulars on the monks; the monks that have more liberty on those that have less; and all of them on the mendicants; the mendicants on the Carthusians, among whom, if anywhere, this piety lies buried, but yet so close that scarce anyone can perceive it. In like manner the popes, the most diligent of all others in gathering in the harvest of money, refer all their apostolical work to the bishops, the bishops to the parsons, the parsons to the vicars, the vicars to their brother mendicants, and they again throw back the care of the flock on those that take the wool.

But it is not my business to sift too narrowly the lives of prelates and priests for fear I seem to have intended rather a satire than an oration, and be thought to tax good princes while I praise the bad. And therefore, what I slightly taught before has been to no other end but that it might appear that there's no man can live pleasantly unless he be initiated to my rites and have me propitious to him. For how can it be otherwise when Fortune, the great directress of all human affairs, and myself are so all one that she was always an enemy to those wise men, and on the contrary so favorable to fools and careless fellows that all things hit luckily to them?

You have heard of that Timotheus, the most fortunate general of the Athenians, of whom came that proverb, "His net caught fish, though he were asleep;" and that "The owl flies;" whereas these others hit properly, wise men "born in the fourth month;" and again, "He rides Sejanus's his horse;" and "gold of Toulouse," signifying thereby the extremity of ill fortune. But I forbear the further threading of proverbs, lest I seem to have pilfered my friend Erasmus' adages. Fortune loves those that have least wit and most confidence and such as like that saying of Caesar, "The die is thrown." But wisdom makes men bashful, which is the reason that those wise men have so little to do, unless it be with poverty, hunger, and chimney corners; that they live such neglected, unknown, and hated lives: whereas fools abound in money, have the chief commands in the commonwealth, and in a word, flourish every way. For if it be happiness to please princes and to be conversant among those golden and diamond gods, what is more unprofitable than wisdom, or what is it these kind of men have, may more justly be censured? If wealth is to be got, how little good at it is that merchant like to do, if following the precepts of wisdom, he should boggle at perjury; or being taken in a lie, blush; or in the least regard the sad scruples of those wise men touching rapine and usury. Again, if a man sue for honors or church preferments, an ass or wild ox shall sooner get them than a wise man. If a man's in love with a young wench, none of the least humors in this comedy, they are wholly addicted to fools and are afraid of a wise man and flee him as they would a scorpion. Lastly, whoever intend to live merry and frolic, shut their doors against wise men and admit anything sooner. In brief, go whither you will, among prelates, princes, judges, magistrates, friends, enemies, from highest to lowest, and you'll find all things done by money; which, as a wise man condemns it, so it takes a special care not to come near him. What shall I say? There is no measure or end of my praises, and yet 'tis fit my oration have an end. And therefore I'll even break off; and yet, before I do it, 'twill not be amiss if I briefly show you that there has not been wanting even great authors that have made me famous, both by their writings and actions, lest perhaps otherwise I may seem to have foolishly pleased myself only, or that the lawyers charge me that I have proved nothing. After their example, therefore, will I allege my proofs, that is to say, nothing to the point.

And first, every man allows this proverb, "That where a man wants matter, he may best frame some." And to this purpose is that verse which we teach children, " 'Tis the greatest wisdom to know when and where to counterfeit the fool." And now judge yourselves what an excellent thing this folly is, whose very counterfeit and semblance only has got such praise from the learned. But more candidly does that fat plump "Epicurean bacon-hog," Horace, for so he calls himself, bid us "mingle our purposes with folly;" and whereas he adds the word bravem, short, perhaps to help out the verse, he might as well have let it alone; and again, " 'Tis a pleasant thing to play the fool in the right season;" and in another place, he had rather "be accounted a dotterel and sot than to be wise and made mouths at." And Telemachus in Homer, whom the poet praises so much, is now and then called nepios, fool: and by the same name, as if there were some good fortune in it, are the tragedians wont to call boys and striplings. And what does that sacred book of Iliads contain but a kind of counter-scuffle between foolish kings and foolish people? Besides, how absolute is that praise that Cicero gives of it! "All things are full of fools." For who does not know that every good, the more diffusive it is, by so much the better it is?

But perhaps their authority may be of small credit among Christians. We'll therefore, if you please, support our praises with some testimonies of Holy Writ also, in the first place, nevertheless, having forespoke our theologians that they'll give us leave to do it without offense. And in the next, forasmuch as we attempt a matter of some difficulty and it may be perhaps a little too saucy to call back again the Muses from Helicon to so great a journey, especially in a matter they are wholly strangers to, it will be more suitable, perhaps, while I play the divine and make my way through such prickly quiddities, that I entreat the soul of Scotus, a thing more bristly than either porcupine or hedgehog, to leave his scorebone awhile and come into my breast, and then let him go whither he pleases, or to the dogs. I could wish also that I might change my countenance, or that I had on the square cap and the cassock, for fear some or other should impeach me of theft as if I had privily rifled our masters' desks in that I have got so much divinity. But it ought not to seem so strange if after so long and intimate an acquaintance and converse with them I have picked up somewhat; when as that fig-tree-god Priapus hearing his owner read certain Greek words took so much notice of them that he got them by heart, and that cock in Lucian by having lived long among men became at last a master of their language.

But to the point under a fortunate direction. Ecclesiastes says in his first chapter, "The number of fools is infinite;" and when he calls it infinite, does he not seem to comprehend all men, unless it be some few whom yet 'tis a question whether any man ever saw? But more ingeniously does Jeremiah in his tenth chapter confess it, saying, "Every man is made a fool through his own wisdom;" attributing wisdom to God alone and leaving folly to all men else, and again, "Let not man glory in his wisdom." And why, good Jeremiah, would you not have a man glory in his wisdom? Because, he'll say, he has none at all. But to return to Ecclesiastes, who, when he cries out, "Vanity of vanities, all is vanity!" what other thoughts had he, do you believe, than that, as I said before, the life of man is nothing else but an interlude of folly? In which he has added one voice more to that justly received praise of Cicero's which I quoted before, viz., "All things are full of fools." Again, that wise preacher that said, "A fool changes as the moon, but a wise man is permanent as the sun," what else did he hint at in it but that all mankind are fools and the name of wise only proper to God? For by the moon interpreters understand human nature, and by the sun, God, the only fountain of light; with which agrees that which Christ himself in the Gospel denies, that anyone is to be called good but one, and that is God. And then if he is a fool that is not wise, and every good man according to the Stoics is a wise man, it is no wonder if all mankind be concluded under folly. Again Solomon, Chapter 15, "Foolishness," says he, "is joy to the fool," thereby plainly confessing that without folly there is no pleasure in life. To which is pertinent that other, "He that increases knowledge, increases grief; and in much understanding there is much indignation." And does he not plainly confess as much, Chapter 7, "The heart of the wise is where sadness is, but the heart of fools follows mirth"? by which you see, he thought it not enough to have learned wisdom without he had added the knowledge of me also. And if you will not believe me, take his own words, Chapter 1, "I gave my heart to know wisdom and knowledge, madness and folly." Where, by the way, 'tis worth your remark that he intended me somewhat extraordinary that he named me last. A preacher wrote it, and this you know is the order among churchmen, that he that is first in dignity comes last in place, as mindful, no doubt, whatever they do in other things, herein at least to observe the evangelical precept.

Besides, that folly is more excellent than wisdom the son of Sirach, whoever he was, clearly witnesses, Chapter 44, whose words, so help me, Hercules! I shall not once utter before you meet my induction with a suitable answer, according to the manner of those in Plato that dispute with Socrates. What things are more proper to be laid up with care, such as are rare and precious, or such as are common and of no account? Why do you give me no answer? Well, though you should dissemble, the Greek proverb will answer for you, "Foul water is thrown out of doors;" which, if any man shall be so ungracious as to condemn, let him know 'tis Aristotle's, the god of our masters. Is there any of you so very a fool as to leave jewels and gold in the street? In truth, I think not; in the most secret part of your house; nor is that enough; if there be any drawer in your iron chests more private than other, there you lay them; but dirt you throw out of doors. And therefore, if you so carefully lay up such things as you value and throw away what's vile and of no worth, is it not plain that wisdom, which he forbids a man to hide, is of less account than folly, which he commands him to cover? Take his own words, "Better is the man that hideth his folly than he that hideth his wisdom." Or what is that, when he attributes an upright mind without craft or malice to a fool, when a wise man the while thinks no man like himself? For so I understand that in his tenth chapter, "A fool walking by the way, being a fool himself, supposes all men to be fools like him." And is it not a sign of great integrity to esteem every man as good as himself, and when there is no one that leans not too much to other way, to be so frank yet as to divide his praises with another? Nor was this great king ashamed of the name when he says of himself that he is more foolish than any man. Nor did Paul, that great doctor of the Gentiles, writing to the Corinthians, unwillingly acknowledge it; "I speak," says he, "like a fool. I am more." As if it could be any dishonor to excel in folly.

But here I meet with a great noise of some that endeavor to peck out the crows' eyes; that is, to blind the doctors of our times and smoke out their eyes with new annotations; among whom my friend Erasmus, whom for honor's sake I often mention, deserves if not the first place yet certainly the second. O most foolish instance, they cry, and well becoming Folly herself! The apostle's meaning was wide enough from what you dream; for he spoke it not in this sense, that he would have them believe him a greater fool than the rest, but when he had said, "They are ministers of Christ, the same am I," and by way of boasting herein had equaled himself with others, he added this by way of correction or checking himself, "I am more," as meaning that he was not only equal to the rest of the apostles in the work of the Gospel, but somewhat superior. And therefore, while he would have this received as a truth, lest nevertheless it might not relish their ears as being spoken with too much arrogance, he foreshortened his argument with the vizard of folly, "I speak like a fool," because he knew it was the prerogative of fools to speak what they like, and that too without offense. Whatever he thought when he wrote this, I leave it to them to discuss; for my own part, I follow those fat, fleshy, and vulgarly approved doctors, with whom, by Jupiter! a great part of the learned had rather err than follow them that understand the tongues, though they are never so much in the right. Not any of them make greater account of those smatterers at Greek than if they were daws. Especially when a no small professor, whose name I wittingly conceal lest those choughs should chatter at me that Greek proverb I have so often mentioned, "an ass at a harp," discoursing magisterially and theologically on this text, "I speak as a fool, I am more," drew a new thesis; and, which without the height of logic he could never have done, made this new subdivision--for I'll give you his own words, not only in form but matter also--"I speak like a fool," that is, if you look upon me as a fool for comparing myself with those false apostles, I shall seem yet a greater fool by esteeming myself before them; though the same person a little after, as forgetting himself, runs off to another matter.

But why do I thus staggeringly defend myself with one single instance? As if it were not the common privilege of divines to stretch heaven, that is Holy Writ, like a cheverel; and when there are many things in St. Paul that thwart themselves, which yet in their proper place do well enough if there be any credit to be given to St. Jerome that was master of five tongues. Such was that of his at Athens when having casually espied the inscription of that altar, he wrested it into an argument to prove the Christian faith, and leaving out all the other words because they made against him, took notice only of the two last, viz., "To the unknown God;" and those too not without some alteration, for the whole inscription was thus: "To the Gods of Asia, Europe, and Africa; To the unknown and strange Gods." And according to his example do the sons of the prophets, who, forcing out here and there four or five expressions and if need be corrupting the sense, wrest it to their own purpose; though what goes before and follows after make nothing to the matter in hand, nay, be quite against it. Which yet they do with so happy an impudence that oftentimes the civilians envy them that faculty.

For what is it in a manner they may not hope for success in, when this great doctor (I had almost bolted out his name, but that I once again stand in fear of the Greek proverb) has made a construction on an expression of Luke, so agreeable to the mind of Christ as are fire and water to one another. For when the last point of danger was at hand, at which time retainers and dependents are wont in a more special manner to attend their protectors, to examine what strength they have, and prepare for the encounter, Christ, intending to take out of his disciples' minds all trust and confidence in such like defense, demands of them whether they wanted anything when he sent them forth so unprovided for a journey that they had neither shoes to defend their feet from the injuries of stones and briars nor the provision of a scrip to preserve them from hunger. And when they had denied that they wanted anything, he adds, "But now, he that hath a bag, let him take it, and likewise a scrip; and he that hath none, let him sell his coat and buy a sword." And now when the sum of all that Christ taught pressed only meekness, suffering, and contempt of life, who does not clearly perceive what he means in this place? to wit, that he might the more disarm his ministers, that neglecting not only shoes and scrip but throwing away their very coat, they might, being in a manner naked, the more readily and with less hindrance take in hand the work of the Gospel, and provide themselves of nothing but a sword, not such as thieves and murderers go up and down with, but the sword of the spirit that pierces the most inward parts, and so cuts off as it were at one blow all earthly affections, that they mind nothing but their duty to God. But see, I pray, whither this famous theologian wrests it. By the sword he interprets defense against persecution, and by the bag sufficient provision to carry it on. As if Christ having altered his mind, in that he sent out his disciples not so royally attended as he should have done, repented himself of his former instructions: or as forgetting that he had said, "Blessed are ye when ye are evil spoken of, despised, and persecuted, etc.," and forbade them to resist evil; for that the meek in spirit, not the proud, are blessed: or, lest remembering, I say, that he had compared them to sparrows and lilies, thereby minding them what small care they should take for the things of this life, was so far now from having them go forth without a sword that he commanded them to get one, though with the sale of their coat, and had rather they should go naked than want a brawling-iron by their sides. And to this, as under the word "sword" he conceives to be comprehended whatever appertains to the repelling of injuries, so under that of "scrip" he takes in whatever is necessary to the support of life. And so does this deep interpreter of the divine meaning bring forth the apostles to preach the doctrine of a crucified Christ, but furnished at all points with lances, slings, quarterstaffs, and bombards; lading them also with bag and baggage, lest perhaps it might not be lawful for them to leave their inn unless they were empty and fasting. Nor does he take the least notice of this, that he so willed the sword to be bought, reprehends it a little after and commands it to be sheathed; and that it was never heard that the apostles ever used or swords or bucklers against the Gentiles, though 'tis likely they had done it, if Christ had ever intended, as this doctor interprets.

There is another, too, whose name out of respect I pass by, a man of no small repute, who from those tents which Habakkuk mentions, "The tents of the land of Midian shall tremble," drew this exposition, that it was prophesied of the skin of Saint Bartholomew who was flayed alive. And why, forsooth, but because those tents were covered with skins? I was lately myself at a theological dispute, for I am often there, where when one was demanding what authority there was in Holy Writ that commands heretics to be convinced by fire rather than reclaimed by argument; a crabbed old fellow, and one whose supercilious gravity spoke him at least a doctor, answered in a great fume that Saint Paul had decreed it, who said, "Reject him that is a heretic, after once or twice admonition." And when he had sundry times, one after another, thundered out the same thing, and most men wondered what ailed the man, at last he explained it thus, making two words of one. "A heretic must be put to death." Some laughed, and yet there wanted not others to whom this exposition seemed plainly theological; which, when some, though those very few, opposed, they cut off the dispute, as we say, with a hatchet, and the credit of so uncontrollable an author. "Pray conceive me," said he, "it is written, 'Thou shalt not suffer a witch to live.' But every heretic bewitches the people; therefore, etc." And now, as many as were present admired the man's wit, and consequently submitted to his decision of the question. Nor came it into any of their heads that that law concerned only fortunetellers, enchanters, and magicians, whom the

Against War and In Praise of Folly

Hebrews call in their tongue "Mecaschephim," witches or sorcerers: for otherwise, perhaps, by the same reason it might as well have extended to fornication and drunkenness.

But I foolishly run on in these matters, though yet there are so many of them that neither Chrysippus, nor Didymus, volumes are large enough to contain them. I would only desire you to consider this, that if so great doctors may be allowed this liberty, you may the more reasonably pardon even me also, a raw, effeminate divine, if I quote not everything so exactly as I should. And so at last I return to Paul. "Ye willingly," says he, "suffer my foolishness," and again, "Take me as a fool," and further, "I speak it not after the Lord, but as it were foolishly," and in another place, "We are fools for Christ's sake." You have heard from how great an author how great praises of folly; and to what other end, but that without doubt he looked upon it as that one thing both necessary and profitable. "If anyone among ye," says he, "seem to be wise, let him be a fool that he may be wise." And in Luke, Jesus called those two disciples with whom he joined himself upon the way, "fools." Nor can I give you any reason why it should seem so strange when Saint Paul imputes a kind of folly even to God himself. "The foolishness of God," says he, "is wiser than men." Though yet I must confess that Origen upon the place denies that this foolishness may be resembled to the uncertain judgment of men; of which kind is, that "the preaching of the cross is to them that perish foolishness."

But why am I so careful to no purpose that I thus run on to prove my matter by so many testimonies? when in those mystical Psalms Christ speaking to the Father says openly, "Thou knowest my foolishness." Nor is it without ground that fools are so acceptable to God. The reason perhaps may be this, that as princes carry a suspicious eye upon those that are over-wise, and consequently hate them--as Caesar did Brutus and Cassius, when he feared not in the least drunken Antony; so Nero, Seneca; and Dionysius, Plato--and on the contrary are delighted in those blunter and unlabored wits, in like manner Christ ever abhors and condemns those wise men and such as put confidence in their own wisdom. And this Paul makes clearly out when he said, "God hath chosen the foolish things of this world," as well knowing it had been impossible to have reformed it by wisdom. Which also he sufficiently declares himself, crying out by the mouth of his prophet, "I will destroy the wisdom of the wise, and cast away the understanding of the prudent."

And again, when Christ gives Him thanks that He had concealed the mystery of salvation from the wise, but revealed it to babes and sucklings, that is to say, fools. For the Greek word for babes is fools, which he opposes to the word wise men. To this appertains that throughout the Gospel you find him ever accusing the Scribes and Pharisees and doctors of the law, but diligently defending the ignorant multitude (for what other is that "Woe to ye Scribes and Pharisees" than woe to you, you wise men?), but seems chiefly delighted in little children, women, and fishers. Besides, among brute beasts he is best pleased with those that have least in them of the foxes' subtlety. And therefore he chose rather to ride upon an ass when, if he had pleased, he might have bestrode the lion without danger. And the Holy Ghost came down in the shape of a dove, not of an eagle or kite. Add to this that in Scripture there is frequent mention of harts, hinds, and lambs; and such as are destined to eternal life are called sheep, than which creature there is not anything more foolish, if we may believe that proverb of Aristotle "sheepish manners," which he tells us is taken from the foolishness of that creature and is used to be applied to dull-headed people and lack-wits. And yet Christ professes to be the shepherd of this flock and is himself delighted with the name of a lamb; according to Saint John, "Behold the Lamb of God!" Of which also there is much mention in the Revelation. And what does all this drive at, but that all mankind are fools--nay, even the very best?

And Christ himself, that he might the better relieve this folly, being the wisdom of the Father, yet in some manner became a fool when taking upon him the nature of man, he was found in shape as a man; as in like manner he was made sin that he might heal sinners. Nor did he work this cure any other way than by the foolishness of the cross and a company of fat apostles, not much better, to whom also he carefully recommended folly but gave them a caution against wisdom and drew them together by the example of little children, lilies, mustard-seed, and sparrows, things senseless and inconsiderable, living only by the dictates of nature and without either craft or care. Besides, when he forbade them to be troubled about what they should say before governors and straightly charged them not to inquire after times and seasons, to wit, that they might not trust to their own wisdom but wholly depend on him. And to the same purpose is it that that great Architect of the World, God, gave man an injunction against his eating of the Tree of Knowledge, as if knowledge were the bane of happiness; according to which also, St. Paul disallows it as puffing up and destructive; whence also St. Bernard seems in my opinion to follow when he interprets that mountain whereon Lucifer had fixed his habitation to be the mountain of knowledge.

Nor perhaps ought I to omit this other argument, that Folly is so gracious above that her errors are only pardoned, those of wise men never. Whence it is that they that ask forgiveness, though they offend never so wittingly, cloak it yet with the excuse of folly. So Aaron, in Numbers, if I mistake not the book, when he sues unto Moses concerning his sister's leprosy, "I beseech thee, my Lord, not to lay this sin upon us, which we have foolishly committed." So Saul makes his excuse of David, "For behold," says he, "I did it foolishly." And again, David himself thus sweetens God, "And therefore I beseech thee, O Lord, to take away the trespass of thy servant, for I have done foolishly," as if he knew there was no pardon to be obtained unless he had colored his offense with folly and ignorance. And stronger is that of Christ upon the cross when he prayed for his enemies, "Father, forgive them," nor does he cover their crime with any other excuse than that of unwittingness--because, says he, "they know not what they do." In like manner Paul, writing to Timothy, "But therefore I obtained mercy, for that I did it ignorantly through unbelief." And what is the meaning of "I did it ignorantly" but that I did it out of folly, not malice? And what of "Therefore I received mercy" but that I had not obtained it had I not been made more allowable through the covert of folly? For us also makes that mystical Psalmist, though I remembered it not in its right place, "Remember not the sins of my youth nor my ignorances." You see what two things he pretends, to wit, youth, whose companion I ever am, and ignorances, and that in the plural number, a number of multitude, whereby we are to understand that there was no small company of them.

But not to run too far in that which is infinite. To speak briefly, all Christian religion seems to have a kind of alliance with folly and in no respect to have any accord with wisdom. Of which if you expect proofs, consider first that boys, old men, women, and fools are more delighted with religious and sacred things than others, and to that purpose are ever next the altars; and this they do by mere impulse of nature. And in the next place, you see that those first founders of it were plain, simple persons and most bitter enemies of learning. Lastly there are no sort of fools seem more out of the way than are these whom the zeal of Christian religion has once swallowed up; so that they waste their estates, neglect injuries, suffer themselves to be cheated, put no difference between friends and enemies, abhor pleasure, are crammed with poverty, watchings, tears, labors, reproaches, loathe life, and wish death above all things; in short, they seem senseless to common understanding, as if their minds lived elsewhere and not in their own bodies; which, what else is it than to be mad? For which reason you must not think it so strange if the apostles seemed to be drunk with new wine, and if Paul appeared to Festus to be mad.

But now, having once gotten on the lion's skin, go to, and I'll show you that this happiness of Christians, which they pursue with so much toil, is nothing else but a kind of madness and folly; far be it that my words should give any offense, rather consider my matter. And first, the Christians and Platonists do as good as agree in this, that the soul is plunged and fettered in the prison of the body, by the grossness of which it is so tied up and hindered that it cannot take a view of or enjoy things as they truly are; and for that cause their master defines philosophy to be a contemplation of death, because it takes off the mind from visible and corporeal objects, than which death does no more. And therefore, as long as the soul uses the organs of the body in that right manner it ought, so long it is said to be in good state and condition; but when, having broken its fetters, it endeavors to get loose and assays, as it were, a flight out of that prison that holds it in, they call it madness; and if this happen through any distemper or indisposition of the organs, then, by the common consent of every man, 'tis downright madness. And yet we see such kind of men foretell things to come, understand tongues and letters they never learned before, and seem, as it were, big with a kind of divinity. Nor is it to be doubted but that it proceeds from hence, that the mind, being somewhat at liberty from the infection of the body, begins to put forth itself in its native vigor. And I conceive 'tis from the same cause that the like often happens to sick men a little before their death, that they discourse in strain above mortality as if they were inspired. Again, if this happens upon the score of religion, though perhaps it may not be the same kind of madness, yet 'tis so near it that a great many men would judge it no better, especially when a few inconsiderable people shall differ from the rest of the world in the whole course of their life. And therefore it fares with them as, according to the fiction of Plato, happens to those that being cooped up in a cave stand gaping with admiration at the shadows of things; and that fugitive who, having broke from them and returning to them again, told them he had seen things truly as they were, and that they were the most mistaken in believing there was nothing but pitiful shadows. For as this wise man pitied and bewailed their palpable madness that were possessed with so gross an error, so they in return laughed at him as a doting fool and cast him out of their company. In like manner the common sort of men chiefly admire those things that are most corporeal and almost believe there is nothing beyond them. Whereas on the contrary, these devout persons, by how much the nearer anything concerns the body, by so much more they neglect it and are wholly hurried away with the contemplation of things invisible. For the one give the first place to riches, the next to their corporeal pleasures, leaving the last place to their soul, which yet most of them do scarce believe, because they can't see it with their eyes. On the contrary, the others first rely wholly on God, the most unchangeable of all things; and next him, yet on this that comes nearest him, they bestow the second on their soul; and lastly, for their body, they neglect that care and condemn and flee money as superfluity that may be well spared; or if they are forced to meddle with any of these things, they do it carelessly and much against their wills, having as if they had it not, and possessing as if they possessed it not.

There are also in each several things several degrees wherein they disagree among themselves. And first as to the senses, though all of them have more or less affinity with the body, yet of these some are more gross and blockish, as tasting, hearing, seeing, smelling, touching; some more removed from the body, as memory, intellect, and the will. And therefore to which of these the mind applies itself, in that lies its force. But holy men, because the whole bent of their minds is taken up with those things that are most repugnant to these grosser senses, they seem brutish and stupid in the common use of them. Whereas on the contrary, the ordinary sort of people are best at these, and can do least at the other; from whence it is, as we have heard, that some of these holy men have by mistake drunk oil for wine. Again, in the affections of the mind, some have a greater commerce with the body than others, as lust, desire of meat and sleep, anger, pride, envy; with which holy men are at irreconcilable enmity, and contrary, the common people think there's no living without them. And lastly there are certain middle kind of affections, and as it were natural to every man, as the love of one's country, children, parents, friends, and to which the common people attribute no small matter; whereas the other strive to pluck them out of their mind: unless insomuch as they arrive to that highest part of the soul, that they love their parents not as parents--for what did they get but the body? though yet we owe it to God, not them--but as good men or women and in whom shines the image of that highest wisdom which alone they call the chiefest good, and out of which, they say, there is nothing to be beloved or desired.

And by the same rule do they measure all things else, so that they make less account of whatever is visible, unless it be altogether contemptible, than of those things which they cannot see. But they say that in Sacraments and other religious duties there is both body and spirit. As in fasting they count it not enough for a man to abstain from eating, which the common people take for an absolute fast, unless there be also a lessening of his depraved affections: as that he be less angry, less proud, than he was wont, that the spirit, being less clogged with its bodily weight, may be the more intent upon heavenly things. In like manner, in the Eucharist, though, say they, it is not to be esteemed the less that 'tis administered with ceremonies, yet of itself 'tis of little effect, if not hurtful, unless that which is spiritual be added to it, to wit, that which is represented under those visible signs. Now the death of Christ is represented by it, which all men, vanquishing, abolishing, and, as it were, burying their carnal affections, ought to express in their lives and conversations that they may grow up to a newness of life and be one with him and the same one among another. This a holy man does, and in this is his only meditation. Whereas on the contrary, the common people think there's no more in that sacrifice than to be present at the altar and crowd next it, to have a noise of words and look upon the ceremonies. Nor in this alone, which we only proposed by way of example, but in all his life, and without hypocrisy, does a holy man fly those things that have any alliance with the body and is wholly ravished with things eternal, invisible, and spiritual. For which cause there's so great contrariety of opinion between them, and that too in everything, that each party thinks the other out of their wits; though that character, in my judgment, better agrees with those holy men than the common people: which yet will be more clear if, as I promised, I briefly show you that that great reward they so much fancy is nothing else but a kind of madness.

And therefore suppose that Plato dreamed of somewhat like it when he called the madness of lovers the most happy condition of all others. For he that's violently in love lives not in his own body but in the thing he loves; and by how much the farther he runs from himself into another, by so much the greater is his pleasure. And then, when the mind strives to rove from its body and does not rightly use its own organs, without doubt you may say 'tis downright madness and not be mistaken, or otherwise what's the meaning of those common sayings, "He does not dwell at home," "Come to yourself," "He's his own man again"? Besides, the more perfect and true his love is, the more pleasant is his madness. And therefore, what is that life hereafter, after which these holy minds so pantingly breathe, like to be? To wit, the spirit shall swallow up the body, as conqueror and more durable; and this it shall do with the greater ease because heretofore, in its lifetime, it had chanced and thinned it into such another nothing as itself. And then the spirit again shall be wonderfully swallowed up by the highest mind, as being more powerful than infinite parts; so that the whole man is to be out of himself nor to be otherwise happy in any respect, but that being stripped of himself, he shall participate of somewhat ineffable from that chiefest good that draws all things into itself. And this happiness though 'tis only then perfected when souls being joined to their former bodies shall be made immortal, yet forasmuch as the life of holy men is nothing but a continued meditation and, as it were, shadow of that life, it so happens that at length they have some taste or relish of it; which, though it be but as the smallest drop in comparison of that fountain of eternal happiness, yet it far surpasses all worldly delight, though all the pleasures of all mankind were all joined together. So much better are things spiritual than things corporeal, and things invisible than things visible; which doubtless is that which the prophet promises: "The eye hath not seen, nor the ear heard, nor has it entered into the heart of man to consider what God has provided for them that love Him." And this is that Mary's better part which is not taken away by change of life, but perfected.

And therefore they that are sensible of it, and few there are to whom this happens, suffer a kind of somewhat little differing from madness; for they utter many things that do not hang together, and that too not after the manner of men but make a kind of sound which they neither heed themselves, nor is it

Desiderius Erasmus

understood by others, and change the whole figure of their countenance, one while jocund, another while dejected, now weeping, then laughing, and again sighing. And when they come to themselves, tell you they know not where they have been, whether in the body or out of the body, or sleeping; nor do they remember what they have heard, seen, spoken, or done, and only know this, as it were in a mist or dream, that they were the most happy while they were so out of their wits. And therefore they are sorry they are come to themselves again and desire nothing more than this kind of madness, to be perpetually mad. And this is a small taste of that future happiness.

    But I forget myself and run beyond my bounds. Though yet, if I shall seem to have spoken anything more boldly or impertinently than I ought, be pleased to consider that not only Folly but a woman said it; remembering in the meantime that Greek proverb, "Sometimes a fool may speak a word in season," unless perhaps you expect an epilogue, but give me leave to tell you you are mistaken if you think I remember anything of what I have said, having foolishly bolted out such a hodgepodge of words. 'Tis an old proverb, "I hate one that remembers what's done over the cup." This is a new one of my own making: I hate a man that remembers what he hears. Wherefore farewell, clap your hands, live and drink lustily, my most excellent disciples of Folly.

    Finis

www.ingramcontent.com/pod-product-compliance
Lightning Source LLC
Chambersburg PA
CBHW032050090426
42744CB00004B/160